Mystical Pens

Practically Magical Poetry

Mystical Pens

Practically Magical Poetry

by Joel Morgan
Mari Scott

www.MysticalPens.com

All rights reserved, including the right of reproduction in whole or in part of any form

Copyright © 2006 by Mystical Pens Poetry
Mystical Pens a division of Mystical Pens Poetry

Edited by Joel Morgan and Mari Scott
Cover Design by Mari Scott

ISBN-978-0-6151-3655-4

Dedication

We, the authors of this poetry collection, modestly dedicate our docile verse to those who have most inspired its creation. First of all we dedicate the life of the work to our heavenly father and loving savior, Jesus Christ. To him we are indebted for the health, wealth, and inspiration that come only from an observant father who daily guides our lives. We are preparing our souls to meet him in the skies.

The mind of this work we dedicate to Tamatha Renee' Scott-Lozano who is herself a solemn and delicate child of inspirational messages and verse. Her pensive disposition, her sanguine voice, and her dreamy eyes melt the icy hearts of all who come within the compass of her brilliant smile. A true blessing to behold...

The soul of this work we dedicate to Christina Leigh Brannan who is the nonpareil when personality and character is sounded. This refined lady has a confident outlook and has erased the word 'can't' from her vocabulary. Nothing is too difficult for this lady to accomplish once she sets her mind to getting it done. A truly worthy lady...

The spirit of this work we dedicate to Nicholas Scott Morgan who has the ability to encourage even the most despondent reject walking the low water mark of life to stand tall. He is never without a smile on his face and a dream in his heart. He is the most amazing young man you could ever hope to grow a friendship with...

The Heart of this work we dedicate to our muses. Many have encouraged our pens and we thank our almighty father in heaven for them. Some have come into our lives and remained while many have moved on to inspire other souls they pass while traveling their personal road. Those who remained will be forever inspirational to us.

Joel Morgan
Mari Scott

Table of Contents

Introduction	page 9
The Mystical Pen	page 11
Upon the Wings of Time	page 12
Mortal Undertow	page 13
Silhouette	page 14
Lonesome Song	page 14
Memory Quilt	page 16
Bales of Hay	page 17
Cloud Burst	page 18
Crimson Droplets	page 20
He and She	page 22
Hymn of Spring	page 23
Dreams	page 24
Arms of Love	page 24
Imagination	page 26
Cold and the Dark	page 27
Leaves Life	page 28
Cowering on the Abyss	page 29
Rays of Heaven	page 29
Slippery Slope	page 30
An Awakening	page 31
Solid Love	page 32
The Horror	page 34
And the Eagle Cried	page 35
The Silent Hero	page 36
The Hovel	page 37
Tree of Love	page 39
Tin Roof Sonata	page 41
Rage	page 41
He Has Arrived	page 42

Table of Contents

Wedding Day	page 44
This Tranquil Place	page 45
Vanity's Fool	page 46
Silky Dawn	page 47
The Garden	page 48
Light	page 50
Love	page 52
Morning Voice	page 52
The Pillar	page 53
The Winding Road to Home	page 53
Rose Clothes	page 54
Red	page 54
Love's Ying and Yang	page 55
Time	page 55
Dismembered Love	page 56
Bottle & Blade	page 58
Mandatory Suicide	page 59
Man in the Box	page 59
Debbie Lynn Again	page 61
These Hands	page 63
Fly my Nightingale	page 64
Thanksgiving Treasure	page 65
Miraculous	page 67
Silky	page 69
River of Dreams	page 70
The Reflection of a Dream	page 71
Love's Fountain	page 72
God's Breath	page 72
Christina Leigh	page 74
An Angel Most Dear	page 74
Earthy Art	page 75
Destiny's Quill	page 75

Table of Contents

Dream Poem	page 76
Miracles and Whispers	page 76
Flowing Eyes	page 77
For Brigitte	page 77
Your Song	page 78
Sweet Mari	page 78
Sadly	page 79
Shy Morning Sun	page 79
The Buoy's Lullaby	page 80
Renee'	page 80
Reflection of a Dream Revisited	page 82
Breathless	page 82
Changes	page 83
Haunted Footsteps	page 84
I Am Poetry	page 84
Christmas	page 85
Stars	page 86
The Gift	page 87
Yellow Brick Road	page 88
Choose Life	page 89
Saint Peter Heard the Bell	page 95
Your Solution	page 96

Mystical Pens

Composition of sundry poems included in this valuable collection has been a loving labor for both poets whose names grace the front cover. Many of the works we have dedicated to our different muses have been included for the entertainment, inspiration, and edification of you: our audience. They have been written in a span that stretches across many years. Many hours of thought and heart went into each piece included.

The difficult part for us was deciding which poems we should include and which to withhold in this, our first collaborative effort. We hope we have chosen wisely and you enjoy each and every verse. We thank you with joyful hearts for spending your time enjoying our works.

Let brotherly love continue. Be not forgetful to entertain strangers: For thereby some have entertained angels unawares. Remember them that are in bonds, as bound with them; and them which suffer adversity, as being yourselves also in the body.
Hebrews 13: 1-3 (KJV)

I can do all things through Christ, which strengthens me.
Philippians 4:13 (KJV)

The Mystical Pen

From my desk lift I my quill
Sharpen its point with the edger
Prop myself before my journal
Scowl at the vanilla ledger

Where did it go, what I sat to pen?
Had something I wanted to say
Did dread clamor dogging my mind
Deliberately lead my lofty muse astray?

Astonishing visions I had seen in dream
When last I slipped into slumber
Are now swamped in a dreary pool
Hardening helplessly as a mighty timber

Should I ford the feral flood again?
Hoping razed memories are refreshed
Or should I attempt to quiet my mind
And reunite with what I was blessed?

I look through gruel pool: repulsive it be
Try to rescue my bantam jewel
Savage shadows obscure my search
And their maddening cries ring cruel

Sullen am I for failing to post
When first my jewel was me given
Again must I mine the murky mire
And recover my alms while still living

I gird up my loins and probe along
Let not cowardice rend us estranged
Lift my eyes 'give me strength I cry!'
That I find my jewel unchanged

Joyfully I spy my forlorn pearl
The one I first sat to record
Eagerly I return with my treasure
And fill my journal with its word

Had I not ignobly lifted off watch
When first my gift was me given
I would not again dredge the mire
And my jewel more quickly be living

Upon the Winds of Time

Upon the winds of time I found you
A lonely man waiting to become
Searching for the love, faith and happiness
Praying for the strength to hold on

Looking for the light through the window
Wanting it to burst into hues of yellow and gold
Wishing upon that forlorn star
Praying for the faith to hold on

Love was drifting through the crevices of time
Looking for its tender home
Searching for its lost soul mate
Praying for the love to hold on

You welcomed life's changing winds
You were so tired of the raging storms
You knew it was a gift from God
Praying for the miracle to hold on

Love reached out her hand to you
Offering you her loving heart
You were bursting with excitement
Praying for the happiness to hold on

Her tender arms holding you
With a soft gentle touch
She awakens your tortured soul
Praying for the wonder to hold on

She floods your heart in sacred places
With joy and peace abound
She watches the guarded gates
Gently go tumbling down...
Whispering to you.... Love hold on...

Mortal Undertow

Apathy, time's vulture, circles 'round pernicious ends
Gnaws impatient talons when she spies stirring within
Patience stays cold hunger 'till the final breath is savored
Then swifter than dirges kisses carrion freshly flavored

Avarice, enameled viper, gold-crusted molten calf
Charms eyes with false prophecy then pegs them to his staff
Deceitfully seducing yellow fools with master's skills
Greedy eyes bulge wildly as forsaken lifeblood stills

Round about Heaven's eye we row
Sailing upon creation's undertow
Sails puffed full cruise a spectral sea
Through this vastness unfolded three

Excess quells the ballad that serenades both mind and soul
Couching home luxuriously lets anxiety become the dole
Too soon pleasing sharps in the most sonorous lay
Grows far too discordant for ornamented fingers to play

Vanity, witless blinder, obstructs Earth's ravishing view
Obscures elegant objects then turns its smoky glass on you
Vanity begins to tremble while walking through occasion's door
When heads that used to turn before do not bother anymore

Round about Heaven's eye we row
Going where? Providence must know
Our wee boat rafts an endless sea
Traveling a course charted by destiny

Anger, whets violent discourse until its razor sharp and quick
Hot blood flogs cold hearts to chaff with misery's crushing stick
Skillfully vexation coils around straightforward logic
Then juices muddled minds with profoundly potent tonic

Envy woos counterfeit eyes then touts them with illusions
Writes delusion into judgment that blisters many millions
Within envy's compass there is no cell for compassion
No repose for alms in hearts whose blood has become ashen

Round about Heaven's eye we row
Jointly as humans we daily grow
Our craft must keep us all afloat
Until for sin our boat is smote

Sadly, blasts from Hell do not blister offending feet
If it were as such many would oftener retreat
Moreover we disguise for our outward show
Then dive head first beguiled into mortal undertow

Silhouette

A black outline of two lovers
In front of a fiery red moon
In a clasping clutch
A dead lock embrace

A black outline of a lonely soldier
In front of a fiery battle line
In a cloud of darkest grief
Trying to survive

A black outline of a lifeless body
Laying in a casket of whitest silk
Finally home
But a wasted life
Silhouette

Lonesome Song

I get so tired of knocking on doors
That no one's hand will open
Swimming down an angry river
Toward an even angrier ocean

Prying open windows
Which have been sealed shut
Walking through fetid mire
Feet stuck in vulgar muck

Searching for love lost
On a littered one-way street
Passing would-be lovers daily
Never yoking the mettle to meet

Every light burns red as I
Travel along my paths

I am invariably the lonesome one
Crossing the finish lines last

I hopelessly attempt to
Out-distance the storm
But the soles of my feet
Are blistered and worn

Searching for encouragement
To placate my life
Endeavoring to weather
Through anguish and strife

I tire of restraining smoldering rage
I crave the warmth of the sun
But I lock away never knowing the day
Concealing tears that make my heart numb

Try as I might to alter my plight
I still wake each morning sadly
Quietly I recite this lonesome song
Wishing I didn't feel so badly

Trying to determine just which one
Of the turns I took was so wrong
Attempting to erase your memory
While I sing this lonesome song

Trying in vain not to love you
The way that I did once before
Still my lonesome heart betrays me
Each time I pass by your door

Trying to sleep the
Whole night through
Just trying desperately
To live without you

I no longer wish to walk
Beneath the shadow of death
Or else my lost love for you
May steal my final breath…

Heavy Sigh

Memory Quilt

Life has rewards: there are gifts for us all
First in the spring then the summer then fall
Each season sews an abiding memory
Every thread's important in life's history

In spring the rose is abloom in the cheek
During summer there are nights without sleep
The fall is the busiest time of them all
In winter one awaits their eternal call

As with a lady of eighty who can no longer yield
No longer can she pluck the daisy from the field
Although her mind is still rich and complete
It will no longer inspire her exhausted feet

However in her mind remain lasting memories
A life filled with honor, reflections, and dreams
Immortalized in portraits to measure the days
Taken to a place that till death she now stays

Numerous particulars are sadly left behind
In the place she now goes there is little room to find
You tell her through tears that for this there is room
However this piece here we will bring to you soon

Arduously you trade her treasures for change
Remove sweet memories that are held in a frame
Dole out riches from the home that she made
Discuss with family on whom these goods should be laid

Then boldly you take her portraits in hand
For the loss of these she could not stand
Binding these sentiments to the cloth from a loom
You create a quilt that will warm her small room

At the top is a man who you will never know
For he took leave of this earth quite some time ago
Next to this is a lady in a print cotton frock
Who admires this man as they pose on a rock

Some of the pictures are of her with a baby
Wholesome offspring of this lovely lady
One taken while on vacation to a sandy beach
One taken that still showed roses in her cheeks

All patched together with stitches and string
A timeless treasure, a most beautiful thing
She is warmed with this when all else is gone
One picture tells a story, another sings a song

So seldom now does she see the world outside
No more parade floats, no more Easter eggs to hide
But still she can recall seasons in her wondrous life
As she lays her head quietly on her memory pillow at night

Each night she is thankful for a life full of graces
When she sees on her quilt so many happy faces
Of the people she has known in her glorious life
Memories quilted strong keep her aged heart warm at night

God has a special gift for those who show emotion
For those who through Christ give a daily devotion
But to those who give comfort to a helpless few
He gives the gift of all of this and more times two

Bales of Hay

What worth we place in noble failure
When we ponder it from a distance
Though hell fire singes our feet
We seek redemption in ignoble silence

Fear need not imprison your mind
Above it your spirit must rise
For it arcs the spine, gutters the brow
And assaults the shine in your eyes

You behave as though mighty barriers
Have been raised along your way
Although if you merely expanded your view
You would see trifling bales of hay

Your mind dries into lint of despair
Thwarted with distorted views
You unwitting allow suspicion
To select the path your feet choose

Your mountains seem insurmountably high
Your vales so disturbingly low
The river that ties them one to the other
Has an exhausting current to row

You discover yourself hiding in shadows
While your existence deteriorates quietly
Your appetite cannot be assuaged
Although your plate is filled generously

Your robust soul screams at your mind
"Why did you choose this way?
Why did you not foresee the burdens?
Your anxiety leads you astray"!

Your survival is taken to slaughter
Though you have the power to overcome
You lay upon yourself savage blows
Your mind mocks your efforts to run

You stand in denial of what has become
Your concessions are crystal clear
However there is no doubt you've succumbed
When your only true enemy was fear

Cloud Burst

She was a sterling lady
Educated and aware
With bands of finest silver
Weaved into her saffron hair
Sapphire eyes flashed
As she danced atop a cloud
Sliding along rainbows
Wearing a mist-blue gossamer shroud

He was a workingman
Obsessed with fancy hopes and dreams
Poetic words are his disguise
He dances and he sings
Still he had the bluest skies
Above him every day
Though the two were very different
Still love found a way

And they grew closer
Led by grace, two blending into one
Weather never threatened
The life of love they had begun

Each night they closed their loving eyes
The other in their arms
When dawn broke they each awoke
And savored passion's charms

Borrowing wings from Venus they flew
Through warm skies of deepest blue
Cirrus clouds drifted lazily by
Their shadows standing a mile high

Then came one cold morning
The Sun decided not to shine
Birds chose not to sing that day
And sheltered in the vine
Their shadows stretched not
Across the land as once before
Their hearts skipped a beat that day
And beat as one no more

Each new day their shadows shrank
As the nimbus cloudbank grew
Would the sun ever blaze again,
Or were their sunny days through?
Wider, higher, and angrier grew
The malevolent storm's expanse
Would all the bands that those two forged
Even have a chance?

Then the clouds burst open
And the rains came down
Washing out the past
Making their futures drown
Turning what they loved once
Into pools of mud
Tearing them in two
Submerging what they loved

Borrowing wings from Venus they flew
Through cold skies of autumn blue
Cumulus clouds whipped hurriedly by
Their shadows shrinking in the sky

Raindrops fell, lightning flashed
Booming thunder rolled
They searched the skies for signs of hope
Struggling to stand bold

They prayed in vain
For mercy drops to begin to fall
Hoping to save what was left
Before they lost it all

When the storm clouds finally broke
There was little to be saved
All about their feet lay pieces
Of the life they'd made
They decided it was best
To set out on different paths
Pride would not allow them
To rebuild from tiny scraps

Ironically the paths they took
Had a capricious way
Of reuniting them in the place
That they had left that day
The lovers held hands
Once again and leaned into the wind
Before they even realized it...
They were soaring through blue skies again

Borrowing wings from Venus they flew
Through warm skies of deepest blue
Cirrus clouds drifted happily by
Their shadows again standing a mile high

Crimson Droplets

O' larceny! O' Felony! O' Murderer!
You're Satan's slave!
In doing your duty
You've taken my beauty
And laid my love in the grave
And left a vacancy
In my complacency
A pitiful life I now lead
You've crippled my feet
I cannot retreat
Nor plant a perennial seed

You tolled a bell
For those envious in hell

And cut short a rewarding life
I'm doomed to tolerate you
Taking lives as you do
Then stealing my wonderful wife
I pleaded for you not
To stock your plot
With my adoration's treasure
Now crimson droplets
Fall from my eye sockets
Enriching your darkened pleasure

She walked sealed beside me
Down life's golden highway
Until she was stolen away
Now I'm left to start again
How does a soul begin to mend?
And start a new life from this day?
I sob every night
Since my splendor took flight
Her vision still warm in my head
I love her and always will
Though nights are cold and still
As I lie alone in my bed

But I have a few things
That I should suggest to you
You only took her from my sight
She still walks beside me
Sings to me every day
And comes to my dreams every night
You set her feet on the path
Gave God his angel back
Your pleasure need not seem so great
Breath may have left her
But her soul is made better
Though you cleaved her life with your hate

I stood by my love
While you cut her rose bud
Holding her tiny hand while I prayed
My tears filled the ocean
My heartbreak would never mend
But beside her forever I stayed
Now I wake each day
As the warm summer fades
Her vision still alive in my head
And wonder how can you do

The things that you do
When you could have taken me instead

He and She

He...
I can't take this he cried

Trying to decide...
My life or my lover, I've tried
Love feels as a disease
It only makes my heart bleed....

She....
My love for you runs deep
Cherish you, in my soul you I will keep
I feel as Jesus, dying in vain
Enduring all this grief and pain

He....
Closes his heart ... sign ... "Can not enter "...
Covered in blood and splinter...
Pleading stay by my side and be my friend
I wish I knew how to twist and to bend

She...
Feels like October 31st, Halloween...
In a black mask... trying not to scream...
Crying trick or treat
Stumbling blindly in the street

He...
He portrays the cold
Lying... she he doesn't need to hold
Pretending it doesn't matter
Their dreams in the wind scattered

She...
Pleading ... love is a gift, cherished from the start
Not like a thorn deep in your heart
Love should be nurtured and taught to grow
Blessing our lives with seeds of grace to sow

He....
We found a miracle in the form of love
For a while I was your White Winged Dove
I want you to know I will always be by your side
Help you stand against the raging tide

She…
Can you hold me close for a while?
Just until my heart once again can smile
And even still
Today...
The moon and sun sets in his hands....

Hymn of Spring

Imbibe very slowly from the goblet of life
Be not stirred to move through it hurriedly
Inhale the fragrance that sweetens your spring
Shouldering time to cherish its beauty

Graciously heed the hymn in your heart
For the lyrics will counsel you safely
Consent for the verse to lift your feet
And your purpose discovered more readily

Cautiously abide the content of your soul
Color your spring in warm hues
Hide you not in the darkness of shadows
Dawdle aimlessly and spring you will lose

Mortally you are here for a blink of an eye
Leave you not with the world unmeasured
Mountains may weather and rivers cry thirst
Save you will leave a surviving impression

Boldly stake the surround of your life
Be you attentive in your pursuits
But nimbly and happily amble in spring
For the winter it cometh to soon

Dreams

I close my eyes and you are there
As a whisper in my dreams
Your gentle breath caresses my skin
As you lay in my arms
I fear to move and break the spell
Of your innocence in slumber
You have captured my heart
And I am helpless in your presence

I stand amazed as I watch you move
With the grace of an angel
My heart jumps, I barely catch my breath
As you smile in my direction
When you look at me tears fill my eyes
As I behold your beauty

Then you awake and
I realize that dreams are fleeting
Love is not that perfect
And life is not like dreams
How I wish that things could stay
As they were when love was new
When promise of life was real
And vows of undying love were sincere

My heart thirsts for words of love
That was not pulled from your lips
But given freely
For a touch or a smile that was unselfish
Or a kiss that was not taken
I would give all that I am
To have love returned as it is given

No, love is not a dream
It is the reality that dreams are made of
And I no longer dream of love

Arms of Love Again

I'm standing on the edge
I feel a cool breeze blow in my hair
The valley is deep and dark
But I know my champion is there

I run so far
But I find my way back to you again
I close my eyes; open my arms
And put my faith in you

And I just begin
Falling in the arms of love again
Yes I'm falling in the arms of love again

This love has surprised us
Taken us on a rainbow glide
I would give up all I own
Just to be there by your side
The time is not right
To others we have vowed to be true
My open heart aches for the love
It needs with you

And here I go again
Falling in the arms of love again
Yes
I'm falling in the Arms of love again...

I pray to God for strength each day
I want to do what is right
But my empty arms keep reaching for you....
Every lonely night
I dream of the moment
I will stand breathless at your touch
Heaven knows my untamed desires
Need you so much...

And I have no choice...
Falling in the arms of love again
Yes
I'm falling in the Arms of love again...

I often catch myself
Silently reciting your name
Wishing I were cradled
Safely in your arms again
But I take comfort knowing
I have you in my heart
Our souls are always together
Even when we are apart

And I won't be whole again until:
I fall into your arms of love again

Imagination

Aye the mind a vast expanse
Where ghosts and goblins gather to dance
Aye malicious demons that hide from the day
But in the mind's meadow they gather to play

Mysterious marvels that are hidden inside
Are sometimes bashful and attempt to hide
But if you watch closely you may see
Everything that might not be

Wear your best costume and play a part
Your mind is safe here as is your heart
There are no limits to what may arise
When you open your mind and close your eyes

There are lightning bolts stuck in the ground
While alien filled starships are landing all around
Green fire burns in a whiskey filled lake
Intoxicated angels laugh while roasting a drake

Peer into a hole through the center of the planet
Jump inside, enjoy the ride, but wax not into a bigot
For there, houses fly through a green colored sky
And citizens are no taller than a bantam bonsai

When it comes time to go, walk barefoot along an orange rainbow
It should lead you to a place that no one else will ever know
If your feet get tired, there are always butterflies
That will flutter safely across user-friendly skies

Park your butterfly on a thundercloud
Walk to the edge and take a look around
Watch as armies are driven into the ocean
By war's casualties that have recently awoken

Here the living pass away and the dead awaken
They are trading spaces in a way that is forsaken
Step off your cloud just behind the storms
Using an umbrella as a mime when he performs

Landing on a home you must quickly race indoors
And become the super hero that everyone adores

As ball lightning rolls underneath a baby's cradle
You swipe her up: save her life, and become a living fable

With your burden lifted, and the hour getting late
It is time to go out on your very first blind date
With little imagination you could easily make her swoon
And ride an elevator of love up to a strawberry moon

Cold and the Dark

They buried my stability that day
I watched as they closed the casket
On my brother's lifeless body

I cried "Oh God give me strength"
As friends offered theirs
I realized
I am alone
I am freezing
I must do this within me

So

Now, here I am....
Crawling through my past
Bleeding from stone and glass
Crawling through all these ruins
Trying to drive, but not crash
Through these memories

Trying to heal
Learning to deal
With all these ruins

I will do that another day
Today

I am going to learn to be
Calculated and cold
I am going to master
The art of being unfeeling

Walking away from him
Felt as death itself
Now I have something to compare

Losing him
Losing you
When I think of the cold and the dark
I now can think of you

Leaves Life

Spring's warm breeze kneads brisk chill from biting air
Trembling infant leaves shelter in stout branches care
Velvety blooms flower beneath a Sun warmed haven
Coddled by sturdy branches luxuriously laden

Valiant boughs protect the meekest of leaves
Greening days of spring vanquish winter's freeze
Night skies flash with fire as seasons swap their shift
Angry tempests often set the slightest leaves adrift

Boldly, stalwart leaves bond tightly to their limb
Refusing to surrender to the force of blistering wind
Enduring through gales fraught with rains and hail
Awaiting calm's coming patient as the nightingale

Basking in warmth beneath the glorious sun
Leaves furnish shade while savory fruit ripens
Shadows and fruit, the tree's generous alms
As bountiful and beneficent as Gilead's balms

Through the sultry summer, green leaves sip sweet mist
Golden fruit grows heavy, as it is sunlight kissed
Leaves bask warmly in gloriously benevolent rays
A symbiotic rapport vital on intemperate days

Shadows reach farther as autumn days grow short
Limbs are plucked bare of the bounty they support
Viridescent leaves darken to a golden tinge
Cooling days posthaste are setting in again

Leaves seasoned crimson soon begin to lose their hold
And curl to the ground now bejeweled with red and gold
This is where seasoned leaves spend their final days
Until gathered into stacks that are then set ablaze

From the deflagration, fragrant plumes arise
But the leaves' final prize is a sparkle in your eyes
Pondering this process we grasp how swiftly life passes
From green then to gold then to red then ashes

Cowering on the Abyss

I am dancing on the edge of the abyss
Its immortal angelic glimmer draws me near
I know all too well
If I take the plunge it would result in
Only truths known by God

There are beauties, and pleasures
Unknown by man
Even though I am drawn
Still I skirt the edge
My destiny is drawing me nearer
Still

I hesitate
Destined to spend an eternity
Without you
Cowering at the edge…
I miss you, and love you
While the rest of my life
Quietly fades away

Rays of Heaven

I began life in a troubled time
Good fortune never seemed to shine
Because my father worked real hard
As a sailor with our shores to guard
He found little time to search for me
While I hid beneath our willow tree

It was just a quiet place
Where I would hide away some days
Chasing shapes as clouds float by
At night star shine filled my watery eye
I learned of life by living free
Beneath our weeping willow tree

But I did not expect to find
A love I'd found like yours and mine
Our whispers floated on a breeze
Winds of love blew through green leaves
And I got down on my knee
Beneath our weeping willow tree

The rays of holy heaven shine
Lighting the path of life divine
How many others had come here
To search for love that did not fear?
And when I feel life buries me
I find ease beneath our willow tree

We found this tree a living place
And forged a bond of loving grace
Devotion that sees my hard days through
Runs deeper than the ocean blue
If ever you cannot find me
Look beneath our willow tree

I will need you there by me
Until my soul has been set free
Death will take me through the door
And I will see your face no more
Say goodbye then bury me
Beneath our willow tree

Do not try to understand
If you have not been there my friend
There are places you will go
A place where hearts in love can grow
Find that place and you will see
Love grows beneath your willow tree

Slippery Slope

Despair dropped hard onto a life disgraced
Little by death's hand appeared erased
Save numerous fragmented shadows left broken
Altruistic discourse that remained unspoken

Over this brittle bier, spill not a tear
Hold your tears; remain serene and clear
A dilatory consort has been spirited abroad
Let stygian horrors now cajole with a prod

The gift of mortality was never held holy
By this soul recently laid in repose so lowly
Though flashing bright eyes and wise with lies
Deceptions he devised were derision in lives

While the God-loving solemnized Ember Days
This unctuous fool drooled in satiety's haze
Laud not this libertine who now lies juxtapose
With monsters skulking down beneath the lowest lows

Appeal not for this embattled soul
Draw deductions from a mind that is whole
Beat not a sock upon this jagged rock
The drop of this cock came like a tick of a clock

Now that he's gone there should be song
For you to sing the whole night long
A song of freedom, a song of hope
For the soul that slid down the slippery slope

An Awakening

Tenderly reaching her hand
The distance through the dark
Seeking his, groping, touching his hand
His soul, his heart
He promised not to be so crude
His words so vulgar, so base
No she said; make my world
More than empty space

Touch my heart; make my hands sweat
Passion here more than real
Turn my world upside down
Quake and tremble, more than still
Give me shudders of passions hot
Let me imagine your lips, here
Your hands warm and strong
Opening my dreams so dear

Let me imagine your lips here
On my own, a sweet sigh
Hear my heart as yours... our thoughts
Movements and desires
I want to feel again the ache and tremors
Your tongue will make
Turn my mind loose to flights of fancy
Come lover: take

Solid Love

Come closer my licentious outlander
Let me see your eyes
The loveliest vision you have ever seen
Lies just over the rise
Walk a bit further. Watch your step!
There you go my love
Just over that hill is all
The beauty you have ever dreamed of

Abide with me this gloomy night
My brave and noble archer
Lay your weapon to the side
You are safe here by my alter
Follow the sound of my feathery voice
You will soon be freed
From the crush of this world's lust
Another you will not need

Though you believe Athena lovely
And for her trade your soul
Merely looking upon her splendor
Has never pleased you in whole
Mold your focus around my visage
You will begin to drink
From a pool of beauty, wherein
Your eye's adoration will sink

Give me your eye; permit me to charm
With my golden hair
Your eyes have never gazed
Upon another vision so fair
Raise your eyes just a bit higher
Your soul will soon be freed....
Adoring my face is all that
A brave warrior ever needs...

There you go; my pretty one
You understand my meaning
Now come my dear and couple
With me in this loving feeling
You, my brave archer
Through dangers cut so very swift
Now raise your candle to beauty
That gives valor his gift

Your eyes must be so very sore
From your time away
Cast them upon my unflawed face
And tonight with me stay
For on this night you shall join
Me in heaven's delight
I will permit your tallow candle
To cut through this cold night

Raise your candle just a bit higher
I think you are ready
I hear your breath quicken
Soon I will hold you steady
Oh yes my love, I feel the glow
Want more to feel your love
Another inch and your eyes will have
All they have dreamed of

Awe my love, my gentle giant
You are now my forever man
Your eyes enjoyed the beauty
That no other lover can…
I will allow you, my champion
To rest your hardened bones
For I have transformed your sinful lusting
Into a pillar of stones

You proved yourself worthy
Of a vision so fair as mine
Now we shall be together
For the rest of time
I take your hand now my, fair man
And kiss your cold, cold cheek
For you are now my one true love
And in stone will forever sleep

Beware the flatterer

The Horror

Rockets blazed over my head that day
Mortars burst round my feet
Bullets brushed past my earlobe
Killing soldiers around me

Deafening blasts so close and cold
Have brought death and me so much closer
Around me lay the bodies of those
Who have already met the collector

Briefly the sound of the cannon fire stops
They're reloading crosses my mind
For there are targets yet to be hit
Unfolded body bags to be lined

And for that moment there I pray
For the shelling to begin again
To drown out the horror that I hear
Ghastly screams from wounded men

And still I keep my rifle barrel high
Aiming at the sight of a flash I saw
If I can stop this one from shooting
I may not have to answer the collector's call

I discharged my duty and marched along
Hoping soon for a surrender
Thought of my wife and child at home
So loving and so tender

My mind racks with thoughts
So many things worth fighting for
Trade my life so Sean Penn
Can trash my work to the floor

The horror that grips me as I kill
This father can hold his child no more
I'm given the right to do what others
Go to the gas chamber for

But still I did as I was told
This reason is clear as glass
For stealing the lives I did that day
While Bill Clinton made another pass

I hid my life from death that day
I hold my manhood high
For on that day when so many did
This father didn't die

Soul survives imprints our brains the things we see the soul retains

And The Eagle Cried

We are the Home of the Brave
Land of the Free
The Melting pot of the World
And the Eagle soar the sky

The Evil did attack
In the form of terror from the sky
Unexpected people were battered
Bruised and slain
The President says we will pass this test
And the People rallied together
Donated, volunteered and served
The Eagle wiped the tears from his eyes
And vowed
Freedom will prevail!

The Eagle said
"My wings have been clipped
Some of my feathers are missing
I might be battered and bandaged
And flying at half mass
But, I am still strong"
The fireman, police and Red Cross came
We will retaliate!

The Eagle grieved
As he held the dead in his wings
Hugging them as he sang
God Bless America, Land that I love
And the People prayed
God, Please! Bless America!
Stand besides us and guide us!
The President sends us to war!
For what!!
Fight terrorism!

The Silent Hero

Yesterday a young soldier died in a war
Fighting for our freedom on a faraway shore
He drove off a dusty road and drown it a lake
Was it his fault, had he made a mistake?

Mystical Pens

This explanation made perfect sense
But not to those who lived in army tents
Why was he there? What was his task?
Did his truck fail or was he driving too fast?

So many questions began to arise
As to why he had closed his eyes
His brothers in arms set out to find
Truth in the clues his passing left behind

They went to the lake where his truck was found
Began to take a thorough inquisitive look around
And saw the place where his truck left the road
They sighed with determination at their heavy load

They saw another set of tracks in the muck
That had went into the lake before the truck
They followed the tracks only to discover
A car in the water that no one had recovered

They couldn't see through the falling mist
So they asked a diver to help in the assist
The diver said when he returned to the shore
Windows were broken but the doors were secure

There were no bodies to be found inside
Windows had been broken on all sides...
The glass was scattered all around
Something had broken it after it went down

Then quietly a family of four began to come down
Crying, wreath in hand, bowing to the ground
Speaking in their native tongue, he saved our life
Rescued us all on that dreaded night

To him our lives we do owe
But we were afraid to tell anyone we know
Because we are the enemy you see
And after he drowned, we had to flee

So we are here with wreath in hand
Placing it upon this scared land
Where a solider had given his life
So we are here to honor him tonight

The Hovel

Once base humanity from me crept,
Under a bridge-way is where I slept
And often times openly wept
For the garden plot I had not kept

More rueful posts I had languished in
Places far worse I have surely been
Even then I yoked strength within
To needle aplomb and wake again

I discovered tranquility near the bottom of a bottle
For serenity is seldom found in a riverbank hovel

In my cavalier world, as I recall
Perceived was I as master of all
But this delusion caused me to crawl
Throughout a particularly dismal fall

For I then let distrust start lashing
And I, innocent victim of such cruel bashing,
Hurled piety, which came down crashing
Onto the floor where it fell thrashing

My corrupted home became a profitless brothel
Fortunate am I there is no depravity in the hovel

I stood shirtless in blinding snow
(Repugnance no Christ child should know)
Poised intractably even though
I had nowhere in this world to go

But I had eked in countless stations
Existing on lean Army rations
While defending unrequited nations
Defiled by tyrant's operations

In exchange for sacrifice on that distant shore
I am allowed to angle outside my hovel door

Mired in puzzlement are my brief days
Bedeviled by way of intoxicated haze
Malevolent mist and morning rays
Bewilder my eyes and lock their gaze

Presently, I begin to labor
Withdraw from the bridge-way with my razor

Set out searching for this day's savior
This is my routine behavior

One is schooled in the art of the grovel
When he finds his head lying on the floor of the hovel

From the riverbank I gather shells
Weave dry reeds into baskets and bells
Moil miserably in neglected dells
Creating crafts to peddle at hotels

I gather together my stock in store
Just as a salesman before he knocks at your door
Approach those cooperative and outpour
Souvenirs along with yarns of bloody war

When one is not drowning in a bottle
There is lots of time to remember in the hovel

"Get back miscreant!" they often say
When I first approach and tip my beret
"Abandon thy cantankerous play
You fright my wife with your ungainly way!"

"Surely sir I ferry no malice,"
Says I to this enormous phallus,
"Though my feet are sore from callus
I too once drank from a crystal chalice

I merely ask that you buy my bauble
That I might heat my frozen hovel"

"Why good man you slash to deep
The price I've set is none too steep
I care not to cause you lost sleep
Fine crafts I sell are yours to keep

I offer not to clean your floor
As a vacuum cleaner salesman drumming your door
My wares here would mean much more
Imagine this basket of flowers on your floor!

It does not look good in my place
In the hovel there is no space for grace."

Regularly, I receive a resplendent 'yes'
People actually enjoy my shells I guess

I treat objection with gracious finesse
But there is no sweeter word spoken than yes

This score is replayed all week long
While fumbling for a footpath to walk along
While drunk, seldom does anything go wrong
I just slam a shot and sing another song

A bindlestiff may wax brilliantly into his beer
But isolated in the hovel there is no one to hear

Liberation has waned into worthless wishing
Until its arrival I'd best continue fishing
And hallucinate about what I'm missing
Conjured by whichever bottle I am kissing

Cytherea's vision sustained me during war
Mighty Ares then winged me home to my door
That winter, however, was no season to adore
And angry gods footed all my hopes to the floor

But I have my shells, my reeds and my bottle
What else would one really need in a hovel?

Tree of Love

Walk upon the green meadow grass
Beside narrow stream so calm
Feel the peace and strength water gives
Let your mind grow stronger there from
Touched by grace a song of life
Is in every enchanting bend
Give of yourself to this tiny brook
And in it find a constant friend

Walk further along and there will be
Traces of love gone by
Lovers who passed this same way
And carved their names in a tree
Love is born here by this water way
As you can clearly see now
I wonder if the bond they found here
Still binds them together somehow

Small churning sounds from this brook
Brings to your mind a stir
Walking past this tiny bend
The earth makes the water turn
As with your life you must be prepared
To change the path you chose
Step over mossy rocks and roots
Keep the earth beneath your toes

Ripples are the breath of the stream
So it breathes faster as it turns
Just as lovers that care for each other
In this place where love's ways are learned
As the stream slips softly around each turn
It loves a part of the Earth
Quenching its thirst: giving it life
Here this tiny stream shows its worth

The stream glides over aged stones
Which are smoothed by the water's touch
And with the brook as its friend
The earth and water form lovers clutch
Just as two that share wounded hearts
Take to this stream as they dream
Binding their love as the earth and brook have
And casting all doubt into the stream

The flowers that grow on the water's edge
Are in need of the hummingbird's love
So they offer their nectar so sweet and pure
To attract the feathered creatures above
As with lovers who give and receive
A never-ending cycle is formed
And when there is harm that befalls the couple
They both for their losses grieve

Walk along this crooked brook
Your love's hand in yours
Lay aside the pain you felt
That you need no longer endure
The Earth and the brook show how love can be
If you listen to them breathe together
So take the knives that have wounded your hearts
And carve your names in that lover's tree

Tin Roof Sonata

We cling together twining amorous arms
Nourished by serenity, and passionate charms
Velvety and soft as a vermillion rose
Moans flower into folk song authored in prose

This evening's sleep for us will not come
Night's candle will flag before sleep shall hum
Shroud we each other within intimate affection
Seeing in our eyes only the other's reflection

And you, the perfectly perfumed rose scented sweet
A bright candle's aurora that comforts with peaceful heat
A celestial body that dulls the most beautiful sky
Heaven's sweet harmony graces both you and I

As daybreak draws near between sighs we hear
Calming rainfall wake the world with cheer
Applause from rain drops sprinkling around
Adds pulse to the rhythm of our hearts' beating sound

This tin roof solo that no minstrel could play
Mollifies disquiet in the most rewarding way
Sleep finally carries us off to fields of green
Together we're blessed more than we have ever been

Rage

Her sign for him says, "Do not enter,
No trespassing allowed".
Desire is having visions of redemptions
She runs against the crowd

Her moon is red with envy
He is confused all around
Her breath is pure and holy
Temptation's lust is her holy ground

Desire has her madness kissed
God, she never wanted anyone like this
He is forbidden yet she cannot... Resist

Her moon is shocked in silent trances
His eyes plead for her to know
But her flesh and body rages
Burning out of his control

She tell her conscience quiet please
She sees Him from the corner of her eye
Conquering will be believing
She lets all consequences die

An urgent fever persist
Desire drips from her lips
Is her reckless heart in this?
Yes!
She will not resist...

Temptation is driving her
He is the forbidden one...
She never wanted anyone like this...
She will not resist....

Ready?
This demon is coming for you...
While evil drips from her lips....
Smiling...
Her, you will not resist...

He Has Arrived

You have always been my man in the midst
The fog has always hid your face from me
But I have always felt you
It is comforting that the Fog has lifted
And you have finally arrived
I will not search anymore

The more I know about you
The more I am convinced
That you are he
My White Winged Dove
The more I learn
The more I have to consume you

I have felt you all my life
I have heard you sing to me

I have seen your love shine through me
I feel as though you have loved my body
But never physically ever touched me

For years
I have not woke happy, looking forward to life
But your existence has brought my soul
Back to life
I feel with you here with me
I can once again be whole
And complete

Whatever ever was missing
Whatever had burdened my soul
For all these years
Has been healed in the form of you
I now know why I have been excited for days
Salvation has come into my soul
My spirit sings out
Whatever place you have in my life

I know that we were destined to meet
We were destined to be together
If it be friends
Or if it be lovers
I know that together
We can over come all the barriers
That has held us back
From reaching our full potential in life

My soul and spirit are so happy
I have written songs all day
With you encouraging me and being by my side
I know that I can reach the stars
And become the woman
God has always wanted me to be
Complete
And free

Change has come
I am no longer looking
For it to come
It has arrived
I am free to fly
I am free to be
Me
Mari
The complete person

With you
I am not insecure
With you
I don't have doubts
I thank God for you
You are my never ending circle
Everyone whom ever touched my life
In a special way
Are you all bundled up into one
You are everything I need

I have had one miracle in my life
In the form of my daughter
Today has been revealed
Those miracles still happen
And I could not go another moment
Without telling you
You are my miracle
I know we belong together
Today
It was all clear and perfect

Wedding Day

My mother guided me for years; my father steered my life
They told me I should take time and find my perfect wife
I did not understand at all just what they said to me
Why would I include another when they gave all I need?

But as I grew, my eyes widened, I began to grasp more things
And I saw gifts they could not give like down from angel's wings
So I set out searching for the blessings they could not give
I began to understand I needed more than them to live

Last year through tears I asked you to set our youthful lives aside
I kneeled before a darling girl who I asked to be my bride
A youth I was when I reached for you oh so long ago
You weathered with me all these months and helped this boy to grow

Now on this day I look at you and realize what they meant
That there was only one on earth that for me was sent
I knew that you were out there and that we would blend one day
My parents spoke truly when they said that youth would pass away

You walked down the aisle a bit uneasy a moment ago
A timeless chapter on our book of treasures will now forever close
I take your hand my graceful bride and place this band upon it
And pledge my world will move around you until death decays its orbit

Awe my love I want you to know and help you understand
That every day I will set out to grow worthy of your hand
Yes, mother told me you were there; that I should look for you
But I had no idea that heaven's angels were helping too

I want at the end of every day for you to be my final sight
To be the last thing that I see when I close my eyes at night
And when I wake to start my day I want to see you there
I want to be the one who brushes through your saffron hair

Many blest days have passed since you agreed to be my wife
So many blest days await us as we begin our life
And I pray that every one will make me feel the way
That I do at this moment on this our wedding day

I pledge to keep you safe my love and grow our binds so strong
To eternally stand beside you when all the world's gone wrong

Together we'll grow
Together we'll know
Together we'll bind
Together we'll find
Secrets we'll share
Confronts we'll bear
Days are sun warmed
Nights will have storms
Mornings will have dew
Every dawn new
Through all of these
I plan to please
And start each day
The very same way
To wake anew
More in love with you

This Tranquil Place

Allow me to encourage tender compassion as hearts embrace
For it increases in warmth as bright sun does on your face
But be aware of cold dangers lurking about this tranquil place

Be prepared to parry when your defenses are in need
Do not tarry when it is time and strike with lightning speed
Many evils tread the globe that seed a bitter weed

In even the most pristine room a spider spins her web
She takes her victim by the throat and leads them to her bed
Be guarded that her silky web does not tangle in your guilty head

As one leak will surely sink the mightiest of ships
A kiss laid on a licentious brow may be tempting the lips
And before you even realize, you are united at the hips

And this will be the end of admiration you have known
Exquisite flowers grow not in a place where weeds are sown
Rather, death is the dreadful wage as poison is repeatedly thrown

Take warning from one who's seen the sin of pernicious lust
You have a moment in the flesh but your heart is left in dust
And everything that you designed is whirled away in the gust

What remains is little more than an empty shell
The seamy side hallow and dull as a broken brass cowbell
And every morning you will rouse to a lonely poisoned hell

And you will question deep inside just what you did so wrong
And pray there is forgiveness for that moment you were not strong
But over and again will you hear that wedding chapel song

For it will haunt your dreams at night the rest of your lifelong

Vanity's Fool

Vanity's fool, looking long inside
Found nowhere else for delusion to hide
Fled pride's playpen where he'd hid away
Ran into the furious night and began to pray

His heart deluded with pride so black
Pitifully braced for a baleful attack
The tortured spirit in him was so dry
That broke at his knees beneath a fiery sky

Not long ago, he was thought of as good
A heart beating descent, as everyone's should
The scourges of perdition gathered to conspire
And exchanged this man's purity for lair of desire

Now his soul retches on the highway of doom
While he begs his tormentors to take his life soon
He no longer arrogantly hides tears of shame
Realizing, too late, Satan's snare was to blame

The load of persuasion that he bore on his back
Made him the pace-setter and leader of the pack
The more laurels he garnered the better he lived
But empty was his soul for its hunger never fed

In buckets teardrops now fell from his eyes
The greed for vainglory had him hypnotized
Until his hungry soul began shaking within
He had not kneeled to purge a single sin

Now beneath a fiery sky and waning gibbous moon
This soulless libertine began to awkwardly swoon
His tormentors stood watch as their quarry purged gore
Exhilarated that vanity's fool would be lost ever more

Fighting against tears to rediscover his pride
He cursed at the way he was feeling inside
Despite the tempest tormenting his head
He bitterly opposed places his ardent soul led

For nothing really changed while he lay on the ground
Piety he did not embrace: his soul still hell-ward bound
All the glory and the pride and pleasures within his mind
Changed a respectable man into a sagacious swine...

For he is as a sow that has his bowel tied in knots
And heaves up the bile that in his stomach rots
But whenever his sore belly feels a benefit within
He turns around and dines upon the gore once again....

Silky Dawn

High above the ocean night's candles begin to fade
Retiring into heaven as the sun sets on his crusade
Stars are tied with ribbons and then neatly tucked away
The melancholy moon beds his light in God's chalet

Heavenly lights trim silky dawn this God-stroked crimson morn
Adorning earthly visions as a resplendent day is born

Silhouetted seagulls glide on puffs of angel's sighs
A concert for despondent spirits, a rose in jaded eyes

A hull mounts wide horizon on a trip through silent seas
Sunbeams dance on swirling crests; aw this is nature's ease
Breeze animates reeds and paints angels on wispy dunes
Morning lovers join nature and sing heavenly tunes

Lamplight flags then waves adieu: his sentry duties done
The wrinkled strand, where land began, turns from gray to golden
Swift and true the night walked through but, oh, the break of dawn
Pales all splendid portraits that god's best masters have drawn

Off in the cold distance hangs a lone beacon of light
To comfort distant mariners who jaunt through haunting night
Peaceful is what comes to mind while looking at it beam
Peaceful and as soothing as God appearing in your dream

Dawn waxes to daybreak as sun glimpses o'er the flood
Pristine as fair flowers that shelter safely in the bud
A million eager diamonds sparkle brightly on curled surge
Time stands politely still as splendors of earth and heaven merge

Clouds drawn to the festival clamor for a better view
Then hotly begin to thunder, as a gossip scolding a shrew
But alas there is dread pleasure in their disarming strains
As the coastline becomes skyline and the sunshine turns to rains

The Garden

My life was in a place in which it had not gone before
I did not know which way to turn I could not find the door
The light was dull, the pathway cluttered: snaring tired feet
One-step forward two steps back get up again repeat

Troubled times befall us all (they say that it builds character)
Makes you stronger, makes you wiser, makes you also faster
Try it alone; you will see there is no one like a friend indeed
To turn on the light, open the door, help you too your feet

I was like that. Yes I was; I did not see an end
To bitter times and endless tears I wanted only a friend
But I met a girl that did so much to make her garden grow
Wondered if the gifts she had would help my mind to know

That there was truth, there were things on which one could count
There was beauty in mother earth that one cannot discount
Wondered if she were the one to set my mind at ease
Wondered if she were the one that I might haply please

Gave her a gift of words that she liked to read so well
About a friend, I had made who caused my heart to swell
Saw in her so many things that seemed to be so pleasing
The gift of thought showed she was fond of soulful thinking

The sweetness in her was like a river that
Flowed with many branches
Giving a drink, giving life
To those whose lives she touches

You are amazing and stay that way
For you are to me, a bay
You add a wealth into my day
That I hope will always stay

You give me hope that I had lost
Pandora's Box without a lock
And give my heart what it had missed
A hand to hold and lips to kiss

On this day you are one year older
Going through life a little bolder
Please take me with you my dear friend
I want to know you till the end

Not just what for me you do
But because of others too
That need you with them do or die
Without you they would heavily sigh

For you have made so many things
With just the touch of your tender hand
You have touched my mind; you have touched my soul
And I am moved by the you I know

You are my friend and I love you dear
For all that you've done for me here
You opened your heart and shared with me
And showed me that there can be

So many things inside a mind
So many things not too kind

But in my heart was not the same
Into it a beauty came

Who touched it with a loving hand
Watered it gently gave it land
Shot me with a loving dart
And grew a garden in my heart

And I thank you for being with me today
And hope with me you'll always stay
To share so many memories with
And touch my garden with your gift

Light

Heat and light...
Mind's morning fog rolls away...
As the rush of rolling water jangles in her ears...
And she trembles...
The mist from the falls chills her as she lies there...
If she cranes her neck
Just right
She can barely make it out...
Quicksilver shimmering water falling...

She lies there...
Bathed in morning sunshine...
And waits for him...
Patiently
Bound...
Because it pleases him
Bound to the four winds...
Pulled taught
Willing...
Captive...
Waiting...
For him to devour

Crystalline form rises from flowing waters...
Circling slowly sunlight glinting madly...
He sees his willing prey...
As the water drips down his flesh
She knows he will drip down her soon
When the time is right
He is going to rain all over her

At the sight of her
His heart...
Rises...
And other flesh...
Rises...
Trembling...
At the thought
Of his mistress
And what they will share...

He descends and she tastes of him...
Drinks deep from her fountain...
Slickly sliding sweetness...
Fills all of him as he savors...
Her...
He teases...
Pleasingly
Down the length of her
Never more than merest...
Brushing...
Touch...
The touch of her gates on his flesh...
Drives his passion still further...
Well beyond his reason...

He takes her...
Fully
Passionately
Deeply
One flesh...
As time dies
So do they ...

Carelessly crashing waves crush them...
Rhythmic pounding screaming shuddering...
Bathing...

Spent...

Softly clinging...
Arms encircling...
Love...
For all time

Even if we never shared again, in this way
Truth of it cannot be denied...

Though moss may grow to cover...
The marks of this deep passing...

Hide the truth...
But the two...
Will always know...
And softly smile...
Bittersweet...
Tears...

Love

Sometimes a whirlwind romance...
Sometimes a courtship...
Sometimes a fire ignited...

Morning Voice

Floating softly as a feather upon a breeze
A voice I hear clearly as if a melody
Effortlessly over sun-warmed air it does glide
Revealing with tenderness how you are feeling inside

Serenading my ears each syllable sweet
Over and again in my mind they repeat
Occasionally a tiny gasp will escape
Sometimes a sigh while your musings take shape

Each phrase delivered with exquisite tone
The most captivating sound I've ever known
Overwhelming inflections mesmerize my ear
Charming and careful, melodious and clear

Demonstrating that your mind is gloriously complete
That you never allow displeasure to interrupt your sleep
Though there are many things to slumber you have taken
Happily you greet the morning sun as you awaken

And I anticipate the words that you might share
My ears await your morning voice's loving care
Soothing and soft a whisper starts my day
"A beautiful good morning dear, I hope you slept okay"

The Pillar

I rode a brave stallion to find you my love
Fought the gentleman's fight
Parried with partisans jousted with thieves
Living the life of a knight

I rode a brave stallion to find you my love
Cast my childish life aside
To lay a wreath at your tender feet
And heaven's beauty stands beside

I rode a brave stallion to find you my love
As a schoolboy I discovered my place
To make the world we have come to adore
As tranquil as the glow on your face

I rode a brave stallion to find you my love
With the gift of you god has blessed me
My journeys have made my body fatigued
I wearily cast all aside...kneel before your feet

I rode a brave stallion to find you my love
To ask that you accept this man
Weathered and weary from life's travail
To offer a love no other can

I rode a brave stallion to find you my love
Dismount my horse to take your hand
Lay my wreath before your feet and pledge
Forever by your side I will stand

Life's hardest journey is the tour of loneliness

The Winding Road to Home

A world-weary wanderer finds his feet on the road
That leads to the place he will always call his home
A patch of peace he finds along the path as he winds
As cold dread is shed and dismay is left behind

Driving past mighty oaks that line the winding road
Living comes much easier as he sheds his heavy load

A whirlwind of cheerful color fills his vision on the road
Childhood revisited, as he smells lawns freshly mowed

Winding along the road he passes white picket fences
Serenity, dropped from heaven, mollifies his defenses
He can't suppress his smile as he winds through a farm
Where horses freely run between the meadow and barn

He knows now that home is just around the bend
That happiness waits for him to step through that door again
No more blurry vision when he looks into the mirror
When he finally makes it home the world seems so much clearer

Tears fall no longer in the joyful home he found
Misguided thoughts his mind will no longer wrap around
Loneliness will never bring a tear in the cold morning
For home is where the heart finds a dock cleat for the mooring

His soul has set out once again to ignite the flame of living
The winding road he left behind waits another sorely grieving
For there will be others who take the winding road to home
And never again feel the pain of living their life alone

Home sweet home

Rose Clothes

Her curvaceous body reclines in seductive repose
In a silken gown that clings and erotically flows
Grosgrain sashes hold it modestly closed
As the timid bud does for a magnificent rose
Tugging firmly on the ends of the bows
I expose my rose from the nose to the toes

Red

Red velvet lips
Red shiny nails
Red silky dress
Red open toed shoes
Red lace and satin undergarments....

I'm stepping out tonight in a
Red limousine....
Looking for a Red Hot Love.....
Laced with a Red Crimson....
Hot burning Desire!

Love's Yin & Yang

Love came to me, saved me, and gave me peace
Love visited, stayed for a while and left me barren

Love opened my sealed heart
With the hope of something new
Love, where are you? Have you deserted me?

With the lips that once cheated, I kissed and forgave
With eyes that once admired, now I only shed tears

My hands crave the feel of yours, entwined
My hands once held you; no they are bare and empty

My wish, my hope, forever loving you, loving us
My prayer...God...please helps me through another day.....

I felt a soul mate within you
You ripped apart my soul from within

Your love became everything; it became all of me...
Your love was everything now; it has forsaken me
~~
Lost within what I thought was my deepest love ever...

Time

Time always moves at the very same pace
Whether I am here or in some faraway place
A pendulum's period, one meter long
Gives measure to the time clock's song

Tic Toc Tic Toc

Every hour there is a musical chime
Another hour passes through the portal of time

Two dozen make for another full day
Another saddened day since you went away

Tic Toc Tic Toc

Time does not take away the pain that is inflicted
For time jaunts indifferently and baggage is illicit
Although wounds healed, still the scars remained
Could time ever really help a shattered soul to mend?

Tic Toc Tic Toc

I pray for the removal of your memory from my mind
That I might move onward through the passageway of time
However, silently, I recall those disturbing sounds
Though I no longer speak of it, your derision still resounds

Tic Toc Tic Toc

For bitter or better, for better or worse
Time sows its seed, spawning its curse
I worry that there is so little left of it
That time will catch up to me
Before I catch up to it....

Tic Toc Tic Toc

Dismembered Love

You do not stand when I come home like you used to anymore
You look not happy at all as I walk through the door
I worked today to bring us things that comfort our nice home
Tomorrow I will do the same so we can keep our phone

But all the same you look content
I wonder why that's so
Is there something you don't want for me to know?
You say that we don't talk any more about what really counts
Our chats are about making money and grocery store discounts

Do these things not matter now? What made you change you way?
I did not even get a glance when I came home today
There are so many things I do to try to make you happy

Wake up at dawn and go to work; feel sacrifice I make
Only to come home late at night and hear of my last mistake

Mystical Pens

You kept yourself so busy with the things you had to do
You did your nails and makeup and you got a new hairdo
And cleverly you found a way to fit into your day
A chance to go and see your friends and laugh your cares away

At whose expense did these laughs come; or were you hypnotized?
Did you find a way to hide these things behind sad eyes?
The tears I see when I come home I hope I've not deserved
You traded our commitment to together fight the world

For club cards and fancy barbs and things not so wholesome
Plant a flower watch it grow you might not feel so lonesome
When we were kids we used to toss a stone into the lake
Just to watch it make a splash and cause an awesome quake

We would choose the smoothest stones that on the bank we'd find
Skip them across the crests until nightfall made us blind
Together we have worked to bring happiness to our door
But the setbacks do not make this joyous anymore

Thus, I sit here with this wonder; how can you be content?
Is there another who understands for what your life was meant?
Is there a charmer out there, dear, that makes your eyelids pulse?
Is there a magic cupid heart that knows how you convulse?

For if there is confess it now and let me go on stride
Do not keep your shame from me I am here on your side
But keep in mind this one thing I do not mind your wishing
There was something you did not have
That thing that you've been missing

Hide your mind, you cannot do; your dreams give you away
For you have called his name at night in a loving, dreamy way
So honor us with truth here and go on with your life
This should not be so hard my dear, after all for you are my wife

If you cannot tell me now then what are we here for?
Just make sure that you tell the kids before you slam the door
That there was no more to do... you did for them so much
That there was nothing left to do that did not make more dust

That you were lonely; there was a loss, which you had to forsake
How much misery must you take? Before your heart begins to break?
Were you to be a sitting duck? Just waiting for your time?
You had to take what you deserved to make what's ours be thine

I just hope that our kids did not really like story time

And lovers love to tussle and tussle till they're bent
But tussling love dismembers lovers and dismembered love is rent

Bottle & Blade

Oh sweet blade we meet again
You glimmer so bright my dearest friend
This time you will love me in a way no one could
If I find in the bottle the courage that I should

Dear sweet bottle my wife and my lover
You give me courage and strength as no other
Though tonight we will eternally part
Know I have loved you with all of my heart

Another sip of courage I take from your warm lips
Then I spy my dearest friend on the table where she sits
I take her in my hand and admire her whetted tip
Hold her to my artery and from the bottle sip

A crimson drop; so close this time
Eternity awaits and peace we shall find
I am yours and you are mine, you see
And this is how it's meant to be

Take another sip of courage; this time will be the end
No more anger, no more tears, no more Judas friend
It will be better just observe and behold
You and I will walk on streets of gold

Blade, it is time for you to take over
For we do not need to get any older
I will lay my head down here and let you do the rest
The bottle has given us courage we must put to the test

We are ready, you and I, just don't loose the nerve
Do your part I will do mine and the bottle will do hers
Let us sleep for a moment it will be okay
A few minutes will not change what we must do today

Oh dear blade you let me sleep through another night
Laid my head down far too long and the morning is so bright

You were ready; I felt your tug, pulling us toward the end
But there was not enough courage in the bottle
And she let us down again

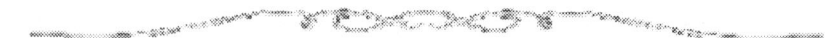

Mandatory Suicide

Last night I was invited
To a Mandatory suicide
The 'vette driving itself towards
Lake Michigan at a dangerous pace
Then by chance
The 'vette steered towards
The sound of the graveyard

As I sat on the bench
By the grave
My heart and soul
Were soothed
By my brothers
Still Voice

Mari, I am your angel
And you are going
To be alright
It is his loss
And right now....
He is regretting his choices

Man in the Box

Blackbird, why do you waste your time?
You know you will fail if you attempt to fly
Blackbird your feathers are as dark as sky
You would blend into night if you try to fly

One often overlooks flowers growing in their garden
Tiny tapestry treasures without care are sure to harden
Many minor mercies are given for you to enjoy.
Waste not wishes wildly like tone-deaf choirboy

Blackbird, sweat not another wasted drop
Your efforts are selfish and meager
Blackbird, the world favors not your kind
Your existence a mockery to the believer

Freely floating figment of the walking dead misguided
Blazes burning brightly dazzle not the narrow sighted
Grace's galleons gave to him a bounty for the taking
Shortsighted simpleton thought healing was elsewhere waiting.

Blackbird, if you have some thing
It was not meant for you
Blackbird! Give it back
Because you are an impish fool

Aggravation assists anguish in stoking the anxious mind
Baldly believing Blackbird's was the only voice that shined
Caustic critics clamored in his brain with lethal voices
Soul shaking sadly for the sore mistaking in his choices

Blackbird, why don't you
Put an end to all your pain
Blackbird, you have naught to lose
The universe to gain

Haunted, homeless, helpless, he heaps sorrow on his back
Looks languidly lonesome toward his the next vicious attack
Slipping skyward slowly, courage ramps inside his mind
Fully finding freedom that in life he could not find

Blackbird you are beginning to see
That you are no longer needed
Blackbird, you take more than give
Your word's no longer heeded

Cockeyed Captain Courage is now laid in endless sleep
Foul fish feast submerged in the sea below a reef
Loneliness left lingering in the world where his soul pined
Blackbird's broken bitterness, is gladly left behind

Blackbird you have done your best
Falling victim to my ploy
Blackbird I must find another
Soul I can annoy

Two thread through the sanctuary's open door
Sharing shoulders six finally cross over the floor
Bearing Blackbird's burden, an indifferent dunce
Many mourners musing, "Why didn't he turn to us just once"?

Debbie Lynn Again

I think of you so often
When I see a child on a spring day at play
I see your face amongst the softest clouds
That float along the way

I hear your name beneath the breezes
That blow oh so softly
They remind me of wondrous times
That I enjoy thinking of dotingly

And I know if I sit silently
I will hear your name ride the wind
And the wind repeats your name to me
Debbie Lynn, Debbie Lynn, Debbie Lynn again

So much stronger have I a love for you
Than the ocean that carves the shore
Slashing and crashing and being held back:
To be kept in the sea evermore

I hear your name from beneath the waves
That whips the shore so strongly
Forsaken was I by your love
When you left my poor heart lonely

If I but listen closely to the sea and shore
Battle an endless war
I hear the waves speak out your name
Debbie Lynn, Debbie Lynn, Debbie Lynn again

So weak I am when thinking of you
Like a lamb that clings to his mother
And I need you with me forever dear
Like the lamb and the ewe need each other

So soft your name is to me
Like the wool of the lamb newly born
But your soft kiss is what I most miss
When without you in the morn

But I know if I sit quiet
In the meadow with the sheep as they dream
The lamb softly bleats your name to me
Debbie Lynn, Debbie Lynn, Debbie Lynn again

I woke this morn before the sun
The stars like diamonds shined
And in sweet heaven's wondrous depth
I saw you beautifully outlined

For I am the compass and you are my star
You point me along my way
And I am lost without you to show
On which path I should stay

When I looked skyward on that morning
I caught the stars while twinkling
And I saw them blink out your name to me
Debbie Lynn, Debbie Lynn, Debbie Lynn again

The angels up in heaven above
Beat their white wings softly
Look down on one they spent much time on
While creating a work so artfully

Their wings beat softly as they
Look so proudly upon the beautiful you
So many splendors on three tiny syllables
And they ring a sonorous tune

I can hear words, if I sit still long enough
From underneath their wings
The angel's wings whisper your name to me
Debbie Lynn Debbie Lynn Debbie Lynn again

When darkness falls and day is done
I close my eyes on the world outside
Then eagerly slip between the sheets
And hope my muse is kind

For on those nights when dreamtime comes
I shall have you in my arms
Then touch your face, kiss your lips
And drink to your amazing charms

And in my dreams I say the words
I want to say until my end
And boldly shout your name so loud
Debbie Lynn, Debbie Lynn, Debbie Lynn again

I know that in the morning

Mystical Pens

When I wake to see a newly fallen day
I shall hear your name in places I go
As I am on about my way

The angels so lovely, the lamb so soft
The ocean so mighty, the stars far from us
All know the beauty you have within
And they each over you make a fuss

And I as well, on this day,
Pull your heart close to mine and sing
And from my lips come the words I love
Debbie Lynn, Debbie Lynn, Debbie Lynn again

And when my final breath is drawn
And my time on this earth is no more
I shall take your vision heavenward
That I am not lost and heart sore

For like honey from the comb
Your name is to me so sweet and oh so wholesome
I know I was blessed for having you here
When I was so very lonesome

Then I shall thank god for whom he sent to Earth
A mentor to wholesome living
Then I shall eternally repeat your name
Debbie Lynn, Debbie Lynn, Debbie Lynn again

These Hands

These hands once held you so very tight
Calmed you when you were scared at night
Pulled the handle of your Radio Flyer
When your hair was wet, they held the dryer

These hands I used to pitch a ball
That you hit against the wall
They clapped proudly when you ran
Held your head up when you swam

These hands I used to write my thoughts
Wrapped Christmas ribbon around a box
Fueled the lamplight, lit its wick
Filled the teaspoon when you were sick

These hands I used at story time
To find a book with the best rhyme
They turned the pages as we read
Then they tucked you into bed

These hands I used to grab your collar
When you did wrong they made you holler
These hands are older now than you
They have touched things aged and new

My hands have done so many things
They've hung nets and they've hung swings
They are my hearts extension to you
And they will always love you true

Keep in mind this one thing
The best place they have ever been
Is in your tiny outstretched hand
When as a child your life began

*Why is it that the good must end
While the bad gets to visit again?*

Fly My Nightingale

How do I surrender what for so long I've held?
Will I ever feel again the things with you I've felt?
I know that too soon the time will arrive
For you to take wing and soar a spacious sky

I want so for you to be a kite on a string
That when there are storms I can fetch you in
And still I want for you to be free
Un-tethered, un-bound, soaring happily

Did I complete with you what I set out to do?
If you falter am I the one to be accused?
I pray that you sensibly considered my plight
Before you set out on your maiden flight

Cautiously I un-bind your velvety feathers
Making sure they can withstand the weather
I coax you to extend them and appraise
Making certain that they will carry your weight

To stay above the ground you will have to fly high
Let the press of the east wind be your ally
As you fly keep the breeze under your wing
Use your honed eyes to take in every thing

Now take a deep breath; I think you are ready
Be not afraid; use your tail to keep you steady
Just grab the next breeze that floats by
And fly my lovely nightingale fly

Thanksgiving Treasure

I hope today is alive with family and friends
And that you together find a love without ends
That today you earn thanks for things you have done
And you return it unto them: each and every one

I hope you find happiness in the eyes of your children
They are the most delightful gift you are ever given
Warm love you see in their eyes snow pure
They do not doubt and their love is sure

You see it in their eyes and again on their faces
Not an instant do they feel that your love is baseless
On this day we give thanks for the gifts we've received
We give back to the givers we give thanks for their deeds

You can see it frequently when a mother holds her son
She shows her thanks for things he has done
You see it in a father when he speaks with his child
He edifies with wisdom; thus she's safe all the while

You feel appreciation when they hug your neck tight
When yours is the name they call on a fitful night
When they show their love there is no hesitation
They give it so freely without reservation

You feel tender love in a friend you have chosen
To share your life with and think of quite often
You feel it when meeting after a very long time
And are warmed knowing you have been on their mind

You can see thanks that a father gives a mother
For the gift of his children he gives thanks to no other

When tears fill their eyes as it comes that time to part
Kiss their cheek softly and take them into your heart

For they will need love to carry them through
For until the next Thanksgiving, they will miss you
On this day when we have so many thanks to give
Be thankful for the life you live

Be thankful for the gifts you're given
Give thanks to those no longer living
Give thanks to god in heaven above
Give thanks for his eternal love

Give thanks to the puppy that wags his tail
When you rub his back and fill his pail
Remember that stranger on this day
Who lent you a hand on the highway

We often take our family for granted
As some have passed and others transplanted
But today we let our hard hearts be raised
To a higher place our loving God has praised

And I, as well, give thanks, my friend
To you for all that you have been
For all the things that you have done
You are a very special one

Our hearts have grown together it seems
And I thank God for what my life now means
I now have you to share Thanksgiving with
As love for you is my most treasured gift

There's a special place in my heart for you
A heart full of happiness for we two
I give you this verse of Thanksgiving treasure
To glad your heart and enjoy at leisure

To tell you that, on this thankful day,
I pray you are blessed in a special way
And I hope that you will always know
That I take you with me where ever I go

You are in my heart you are in my mind
And I thank god for you at this Thanksgiving time

So many Christmases were like this you see,
And I want them all this way for you, my dear family.

Miraculous

What a miraculous time to relax and recall
The seasons in my life that I cherished above of all
Though white winter chills and eager air blows cold
I am warmed when recalling holiday memories of old

Heavenly miracles made my peaceful eyes grow wide
Those graces, then so simple, now casts misery aside
I never considered that blooms could wilt in such a season
Looking back on all those things that were so very pleasing

While in school I would fold notebook paper pie shaped
Carefully cut away small pieces to create a snowflake
Then hurry home to hang it on our Christmas tree
Glance about to see if there was another gift for me

Mother would make sweet cocoa piping hot
Delicate marshmallows turned to cream at the top
I would sneak up behind and grab her round her waist
She would twirl to see a cocoa smile bloom on my face

She would have many things cooking on her stove
And on the kitchen table sat a needle, thread, and bow
I knew what that meant: it was time to bring
Popcorn from the stovetop to thread onto the string

So I fetched a large bowl and filled it to the top
From the tin foil dome puffed full of Jiffy Pop
Then mother and I laced a popcorn vine
To hang upon the maple for winter birds to find

When it was strung I would bear it outside
So hungry could also enjoy this Yuletide
Then we would clear foggy windows to see
Cheerful birds arrive to feast from the popcorn tree

My cheeks, now ablaze, had flushed from winter air
I warm near the hearth alive with fire's flare
Removing my sweater my boots and my hood
I would help make delicacies that tasted so good

We would start by making tasty Christmas goodies
Carmel candy apples and chocolate chip cookies

Honey topped bread savory, warm, and pleasing
Velvet cake decorated with red and green icing

Then honeyed ham from its skewer was removed
A choice holiday entrée', which was by all approved
Mother seeing amazement bubble in my face
Gave me the mixing bowl from which to steal a taste

Oh how I wished that there was never an end
To the spirit of the season that was directed in
Not to be outdone by joy blooming in the kitchen
Papa would don his Santa suit and sneak in

And he would say in a Santa like way
"Ho! Ho! Ho! Have you been being good today?"
"Oh Yes Santa you should be so very proud of me
For I made the snow birds a popcorn tree"

Then Santa would start with singing a song
Happily my mother and I would carol along
We would set the table then thank God for his grace
Grateful were we all for love washing through this place

Magical love drops filled our family's flowing cup
Of enmity, there was naught so much as a dollop
Resounding memories shall live forever in my mind
A more cheerful time I am likely not to find

So my Christmas's were like that you see
I want them this way for you, my dear family

And when my grandchildren are finally here
I want to tell them about this most miraculous
Time of year...
Each of you...
Miraculous in your own creative way...

Silky

Nap my lovely, dream peacefully; soothe your soul with angels
That spins a tapestry of illusions from the yarn of many spindles
You are now in an exquisite place with a warm glow on your face
I observe your slumber from the threshold as you dream in a bed of lace

Mystical Pens

I see your lips move a bit as with angels in your dream you speak
My heart yearns to be there beside you when you discover something unique
Merely admiring, as you in wonder dream, binds my spirit to you so much
Wish I could express to you how often my heart is moved by your tender touch

I notice a dove land on the sash and hearken as she begins to coo
I worry that she might get too loud and unknowingly awaken you
But then I remember that I had observed that bird in the garden one day
And she was watching you just like that when you were in the yard at play

I surmise that she like me adores being so much closer to you dear
For we both know that as you dream there is nothing you need ever fear
I tread toward your bed now dear and wrap your silky bedspread tight
Kiss you on your forehead and pray you have a restful night

I hesitate as I step away from you my darling angel
On earth God has sent no one that could ever be your equal
I dawdle here although you well know I too must take my rest
But the moments that I watch you sleep are always among my best

I close my eyes and hope I see you in my dream tonight
I hope my father joins us as our spirits take their flight
Together we will take a trip upon the wings of a dove
And I will reveal that, above all things, this is what I love

I love you when you sleep at night
I love you when you hold me tight
I love you when there is pain
I love you in the pouring rain
I love you when you hug my waist
I love your tears when salt I taste
I love you when there is a mist
I love you when your cheek I've kissed
I cannot tell you more that this
There are some things I have missed
But never forget one thing that's true
I do now and will forever love you...

River of Dreams

Happily you begin your nocturnal journey
On the river of dreams
For these few serendipitous hours
You may become many things

Transcendental ships deliver you to shores

Of mystical undiscovered lands
For this short time you are a pioneer
Taking destiny into your hands

With an oracle's eye you unmask mystery
For here your soul is unbound
The wings of Mars take you to heaven
Just to take a look around

Then instantly it changes: this peaceful view
Dare not you ask for no one will tell
Why you fell from the gates of heaven
And are now staring at the axis of hell

As if snatched from a speeding train
You sit straight up in your bed
Clutching a raging heart in your hands
Alarmed by the things going on in your head

Fitfully you struggle back into slumber
Hoping for a more peaceful dream
Perhaps this time you will dance with a princess
And caress her into an astonishing scream

Here, in this place, you may see anything
Lions that lecture in human tone
Leafy cherry trees made of pure gold
Flowers that germinate on an aging tombstone

Often you want to take with you
The things that in dream you have every night
An existence that is taken to heights unknown
One night you find happiness the next pure fright

On the river of dreams you can do anything
You drift along the tide and soar across the sky
Have a talk with angels
Find out what makes them cry

You begin your journey by closing your eyes
Soon you experience the floating feeling
Shortly the most perfect dream will arrive
And your soul will soon be healing

Take time to develop the most fulfilling dream
Make it a part of your nature

The inspiration that you are given there
Will help your soul to mature

If you are unhappy with the dreams you are given
It may be because of the life you are living

The Reflection of a Dream

Looking into your eyes I see a dream
A reflection from the light in your soul
I know the sands of time will not wait
But on our love it will never toll

The vision of you fans an ever-burning flame
Which moonbeams cannot outshine
It may move oceans and on darkness shed light
But a loving candle's glow is with us for all time

The compass is moved by the strength of the earth
The stars are lit by the sun
But the love I feel for you is so strong
It can by no force be ever undone

I touch your cheek and kiss your lips
Glistening from the shine of the moon
And know in my heart that no angel in heaven
Could look quite so lovely as you

Our love will not by the scythe of time
Be brought to bear contempt
For I love you more each passing day
And is by no raging tempest bent

When we must be apart I pray
That the angels watch over your heart
For you take a piece of me there with you
So that we are never truly apart

I look deeply into the shine of your eyes
I imprint each moment on my brain
So when my immortal soul sheds this body
Your vision my vital force shall retain

When the tides overtake the earth one day
And there are no more tomorrows
I will still be in love with you dear
And all of heaven's happiness will be ours

Love's Fountain

An indescribable joy that is warmer than the sun
Comes from living life with affinity for just one
Which magnifies tranquility deep down inside.
You walk with confidence: fulfillment in each stride

An early morning caress seals a smile onto your face
A tender morning kiss is the first sweet thing you taste
In prayer you praise the divine pleasure that you hold
Joy spices your essence; devotion makes you bold

Each new morning brings fresh blossoms to your love
A love that is watered by caring hands of those above
Each day your valor scales the incline of Heart Mountain
Your thirst is assuaged by water from love's fountain

Two who are predestined to discover one another
Find no fear in speaking what their heart says to the other
What they build together could be neither bought nor sold
And they will have eternally each the other's hand to hold.

If it were meant not to be it would quickly fall apart
The two might go on living but would never share a heart
Your soul's companion is one that God sent here just for you
When you find that someone, you will drink from love's fountain too

God's Breath

Unpredictable fingers grapple pointlessly for fodder,
Frauds gleaned from moist caresses are mere routine,
Masquerading faces, lo! Look on the devils daughter,
Smoothly, feints do alter; never twice the same is seen.

Tongues wag between jaws: slogging 'bout in mire,
Beware the wound of these despondent vipers.

Mystical Pens

Lips flatter like hustler's con; let fire brand the liar!
Collect mouths, for the love of god, as bull's-eyes for snipers!

Fickle feet tread many paths; one wonders why they ache,
Try, for once, just standing still this rest would do you good.
Capricious arms, they wrap so sprightly around a huge mistake
Feels like they have grabbed a prickly cactus instead of sturdy wood

Bewildered heads swag and wonder about where to rest in peace
Forever whirling toward the rear: sensing malice follows close
Backs are scared with countless wounds, earned in this short life lease;
Blame falls upon squalling eyes, muddied thick with earthly woes.

Thus, on what may one depend in a world sown with suspicious tricks?
Have we reluctantly waved goodbye to our God-sent desire to trust?
One wonders why the world is filled with such lewd skeptics,
Disturbingly; to live with uncertainty is something we all must.

Alas, there is breath gliding through air like fabric through a loom,
This unswerving saint moves free; prospecting through heaven's hope,
Look more closely at the heartbeat which first awakens in the womb,
These ethereal constants God gave to level the steepest slope.

Thus for breath, give thanks to God: as in prayer is it best used.
Because breath consistently flows inside until your soul goes home.
Feel your heartbeat move your blood, as to stop it has refused,
Bless the day these heroes cease, through God's house your soul will roam!

Christina Leigh

Cytheria's graces settled upon one
Hardly a blemish stains her lovely skin
Rejoice for radiance that humbles the Sun
Inspires flash fires that burn from within
Spring's task at last, for a lass, is complete
Time winged her sprightly through tender ages
Improving life for each soul she did meet
Never has charm paid more wealthy wages
A lass most praiseworthy and pristine
Lo! She was a babe but a weekend ago
Enticing, divine, bearing noble mien
Imagination crisp as new-falling snow
       Gentle sweet one youth's album now closes
       Haply go slow and smell all red roses

An Angel Most Dear

From Saint Peter's eye fell a tear of gold
Moved by a departing angel most dear
"She most strew miracles" thus was he told
"Despondent hearts storm while she remains here
She'll stand as guide to pilgrims on the flood
She shall pour tears as she masters our plan
Then shall stand witness to soul saving blood
That God planned it all before time began
She will be tossed and besieged on a wave
This shall prepare her for what she must share
For this toil shall serve to make her wings brave
She shall herd flocks into our loving care
       And as a buoy suffer near the brink
       Anchored to faith shall waft but never sink"

Earthly Art

You lie there so still O' my earthly art
While my soul prays that you open your eyes
God sowed a vast stretch of love in your heart
In that fair field all of my faith now lies
Thou art my tender piece of heaven above
My heart prays for thy passion to arise
Living this life seems senseless without love
Thine eyes are deep sighs in my grieving skies
As a boy I dreamed of how we would glide
Along crisp autumn breeze with fallen leaves
Then I turned this tempest into my bride
And to this bright angel all my love cleaves,
    Within God's brilliance are things divine hid?
    I found divine ground behind your eyelid

Destiny's Quill

Measured against the fairest bloom that grows
That sprinkles love mist in admiring eyes
That cheered wide welkin as a bright sun rose
Adorns many morns dazzling whimsical skies
Dignity is with Nature's best quill writ
She composed a fine score when she drew
Everything beautiful the bright sun lit
And blended all of that hue into you
And oh what treasure was hewn out there
A flower laced brook twisting through green knolls
A flawless gem cut with a master's care
With eyes to the skies though loud thunder rolls
    This, all of this, sewn snug with silken strands
    From her nose to toes most graciously stands

Dream Poem

If I could one flower of words create
And no other ink runs through my dry pen
That poem would suspend our parting date
That poem would at once all hardship end
I'd trowel words into wounds with sterling speech
Craft a child's prayer that would make Satan weep
Into each wounded heart would that prayer reach
Trough cloudy eyes no other tear would seep
Mornings would be merry, sundown a dream
Heartbreak and goodbyes a part of the past
My love-struck psalm would all sorrow redeem
And all God's children live in peace at last
      And this dream poem, all the world would say
      Rescues lost smiles and soothes the saddest day

Miracles and Whispers

In the span of a blink life's course is changed
A whispered word freezes breath in your chest
A lifetime of plans must be rearranged
Few things snuggle you into peaceful rest
Nightly you kneel praying miracles fall
While tears chase rosy blush from salt stained cheeks
Pray sweet heaven weaves a miracle shawl
To shield you against biting cold that wreaks
Miracles are like mist, smaller than tears
They come in like whispers: nervous at first
But a heart knows when a miracle appears
For they are life's wine that quenches all thirst
      Then, give hope a dock cleat on which to moor
      May miracles rain down while whispers roar

Flowing Eyes

Sleep well, bright angel, this rest you have earned
Fear no more; you've captured Christ's peace at last
Through your show of bravery we all have learned
That life's banquet is a copious repast
Weep no more, dear, due to frustrating stops
Those tears you've shed have to heaven led
We follow the trail you left with those drops
With flowing eyes we flood the road you've tread
Grieve no more, dear, you have shown us a path
This we shall follow when our time to go
We are each marked and will endure such wrath
Then, reunited, will a glad stream flow
        We all know heaven's just a prayer away
        We pray to say that we miss you each day

For Brigette

How tedious this life we lead seems now
God's grace cut fresh such a darling bloom
Yet before almighty we jointly vow
To recall her smile till the crack of doom
God lent her to us grace, beauty, and fair
And she showed a sluggish sun how to shine
With her radiant soul and golden hair
Who in each blink lived as lady divine
Those of us who have still power to pray
Shall close our eyes and see only her smile
And weep for her loss on this dreadful day
But know that her life was a life worthwhile
        For each day she lived was a life brand new
        While a storm through her tender body flew

Your Song

Your song I knew from sundry rhymes spoken
Your heart I knew from slight cracks in your voice
Honor stood tall its strong skin unbroken
In all your virtues did good God rejoice
Selfless you are in following your church
Holding your love for God higher than all
Love for your close friends was stronger than birch
Beneath the load of fierce earth, you stand tall
In you I found what I dreamed in my heart
The most lauded sight I have ever been 'round
A child to nature; a true work of art
In a pool called beauty my vision drowned
       In all this wide world and heaven so high
       To you, dear, will I my happiness tie

Sweet Mari

Golden locks lay atop a brilliant crown
A stray strand tucked behind her tender ear
Her smile as bright as a gleaming sundown
A mind most dazzling with no cause for fear
God's mighty hand chiseled her perfect nose
Tiny ripples break over her smooth brow
On her cheek blooms a magnificent rose
Ideal for a ball or Hawaiian luau
Her eyes flash as she dances at midnight
Swaying beneath a waxing gibbous moon
Mirrored pools fuel the lamplight of delight
And her movement would make a parson swoon
       Fairest of fair seized from riches of earth
       Still more to adore lies in Sweet Mari's worth

Sadly

Startled by sunrise chorus warbling at dawn
Swollen eyes dart about distorted gloom
Sadly touch a pillow your sweet head laid upon
Salt tear soaking linen again damp as a tomb
Anon! Anon! My beloved fawn has gone
Angels cleaved heart's dream from my side
Alack! Thence to heaven my beauty was drawn
As a bitter sun vaporizing virile tide
Dirge's refrain silenced so long ago now
Days aged to weeks and then years
Drawing more fret lines on my brow
Damning me to ache through endless night tears
    Lo! There is a star outside the windowpane
    Yes my love high above, I am missing you again

Shy Morning Sun

Think of my love but as shy morning sun
Spreading blushing beams over oceans deep
My journey toward love is anew begun
Glowing passion wakes creation from sleep
Yet I fly high but to brighten your eyes
To shine faithfully above splendor's rose
Spread timid rays over earth's divine prize
Warming the heart of the woman I chose
Over mountains and high hilltops I peek
Scattering light over meadows and glens
Yet embrace only the supreme and unique
From morning's blush until evening's glow ends
    Then sink happily below Earth's distant rim
    At dawn I rise, seeking fair eyes again

The Buoy's Lullaby

May sweet sleep sheath your world-weary eyes
Let heaven shield you from harm and fear
When your dreams cease and you at dawn arise
May Lark's sweet song your awakening cheer
While you toward God's love move ever nearer
There is first a broken world you must mend
May grace embrace your dignity dearer
Grant you strength to those forsaken defend
I pray that you wake on a world repaired
Let mirth imbue every creature on earth
And those you love understand why you cared
May those worthy enjoy your alms and worth
    Struggling for themselves some souls would not dare
    Till god saw fit to knit them to your care

Renee'

I close my eyes and I remember that day
You came into the world, a miracle I would say
I prayed for you so many good and perfect things
Your life has surpassed more than golden rings

As a mother giving birth, to her child, knows pain
I glanced upon your face, my joy returned again
They laid you in my arms, so dear to my heart
I thanked God for you, a precious gift at the start

Over the years I have watched you grow
Planting seeds of love and hope wherever you go
The young lady you are, my heart swell with pride
I am blessed above many, you are by my side

I am proud of the woman you have grown to be
To watch you smile brings me perfect glee
I watch faces light up as you enter a room
The joy you bring us stifles any gloom

Your beauty is something to admire
The silk of your hair, skin like an amber fire
Others are attracted to that wonderful smile
Wishing to be like you all the while

But those of us who know you well
Knows your fiber runs deep, we can tell
There is more than the eye can see
That is why you are special, especially to me

I admire the way you love with your soul
How you care for the many whom are old
How truth to you means your whole life
You keep your word regardless the strife

I watch you with a child in your arms
How you love and protect them from harm
You work with such diligence and speed
Your character is strong, never any heed

Your smile and a warm touch calms those who fear
Assuring you will stand with them, always be near

The many you have brought home all those nights
Giving them peace, a bed till the morning light

The many hours of missionary work on the field.
Protecting, caring, and making them renew their will.
I see God threaded through your life as Lord.
I know your faith, joy and love is your sword

You have a forgiving spirit, it shines like gold
You know how to say you're sorry, and never hold
A grudge like most, your spirit is always sweet
Know not a stranger, always willing to greet

Renee', you are my daughter, a priceless pearl
I thank God everyday, you are in our world
I cherish the day you were born with fondness
On May 18th I surely was blessed

Reflection of a Dream Revisited

Looking into her eyes he sees a reflection of a dream
Of a fantasy
Soaring on the winds of time…
Guided by a force they can not direct
Only follow …

His Knees bend softly to the floor
At the sound of her voice
He is lifted by angel's wings
Guided by moon beams of yellow and gold…

He moves and molds his body close to hers
Soaring they move as one
He kisses her velvet, glistening, parted lips
Souls dancing in this circle of time…

He whispers, baby, love is within our reach
As he tenderly leans against her cheek
Time cannot toll their love
It was made in heavens design …

Love is fueled by the tides
The earth tries to cool their lovers flame
But drench their love, No mortal can
They stand solid as time wears away…

Breathless

I see you ……just a glance and you smile at me
I turn again, our eyes meet and our souls whisper
To each other words never spoken
I walk on but your presence beckons me back
With a longing of forgotten love
Our lives were destined to meet…

I stand close to you to hear your voice
And the sound saturates my being like a song
I listen to you speak and every syllable
Quickens my heart until I feel it pound in my chest
I try to leave but cannot compel myself to move
As if it was my purpose to stand by you
Our paths were meant to cross…

Your hand brushes against me
And passion overwhelms me like a flood
It was at that very moment I knew
At that very moment I understood
It was all clear now
We were never meant to be strangers
We were predestined to meet
Our lives would be forever intertwined
Never again would we ever know loneliness
Though our paths were so different
So far apart they led us to this one place
This one moment
This one purpose
I stood Breathless

Changes

Seems lately this life of mine has been going through a lot of changes
Like leaves changing from summer to fall
Everyone a defining moment in time
Sometimes to the limb we fall, other times
We are grasping for life, not to fall
What are we clinging to?
We don't know!
But freedom does take its toll

The leaves change from green to gold to red to brown
Just like your loss of love has changed me
The colors of fall renew our hearts
Souls and minds
But
Love changes through space and time
Yes, we have been through some change
Was it our choice?
No!

Changes…
Of the past, present and future with the fall dew
Keeping the earth moist
The leaves are a design of our lives
Just like the seasons
An echoing voice…

Haunted Footsteps

Deep in the mansion haunted footsteps crept
Climbing the wretched stairway of doom
Time's tedious jaunt was by a clock kept
In dead air hung foulness of stale perfume
She climbed the stairs in her gown of white
Supposing that her lover would woo
Outrage grew heavy on an ancient night
From jealous rage hostility grew
For he was a man who thought her untrue
And his knotted stomach would not be still
He whispered "I have a surprise for you"
Striking in anger his bride he did kill
        Her spirit now climbs those steps every night
        A dart in her heart wearing her gown of white

Art is an innate drive that can seize
A person and make him the instrument.
Sometimes we sacrifice all for our art.
Let me introduce you to our art... Poetry...

I Am Poetry

My name is Poetry; I've lived since ancient time
I bind thoughts together and create the perfect rhyme
I am the articulation of the most perfect rose
When I describe how it smells, I may also be prose

I am sometimes turned into the heartbeat of a song
I can tell you when someone has done you wrong
I stand the tallest among my more diminutive peers
I wear robes of finest gold; I am the melody in you ears

I am Poetry; God's gift of enduring Passion
I am Poetry; my style is always in fashion
I am Poetry; I am the gift you give your love
I am Poetry; your white winged dove

I am Poetry; imagination flowing through a mystical pen...
I am Poetry; I am the words of love that you send
I am Poetry; I am your whore down on her knees
Bridle my passion and do with me as you please

I am Poetry; I am the inspiration for you dreams
I excite your lover like no one has ever seen
I am Poetry; the guilding of the spoken word
Knight draped in armor, shining edge of his mighty sword

I am Poetry; I am the light house for sailors at sea
I will guide you on your way...put your faith in me
I am Poetry; the psalms of the kings
I am Poetry; a crown of thorns that stings

I am Poetry; I am your Goddess in the night
I am Poetry; I am your eagle in flight
I am Poetry; I am the words that make you free
I am Poetry; you can always count on me...

My name is Poetry; you can find me in the spring
My name is Poetry; hear the songs the birds sing,
My name is Poetry; I am the words that you share
My name is Poetry, Look for me everywhere…
I'll be right there!

Christmas

In this Season of Yuletide
Our wishes are many, far and wide
Family and friends and people I've met
Being with loved ones is our best bet

To people we've met
You bring us great joy
Enjoy this Christmas Season
Whether you're a girl or a boy

Each of you are special
In your own way
Our home is yours
We wish you could stay!

Glad Tidings from us
Is what you will hear
Have a Merry Christmas
And a Great New Year!

To each and all
We have come to know

May your Christmas always be white
Serene with snow

We all have ones
That we hold dear
Again to each of you
 Merry Christmas,
And a Great and Happy New Year!

Stars

Looking out across the Western Caribbean tonight, my love
I wonder where you are, and what you are doing
Are your thoughts of me, as you look towards the stars above?
Are you missing me as I as much as I you?

The cool gentle breeze off the Cayman Islands dance
Across the shimmering glow of the sea
I feel your presence with me as I sit in this trance
Memorized by reminiscences of your loving touch

I feel myself falling into a deep, restful, peaceful sleep
As I see you reach out your amorous hands to me
I am so much more than complete
Since you have adorned your life with mine

You are my white winged dove, my moon, and my sky
Your are my stable, you are my endurance
You are my fortress when unsettled emotions run high
I am not your strength, as you say, you are mine

I hear you whisper in my remembering heart
I have loved you from the very start

"It is not what I say that proves my love for you
Look deep into my soul, you will see it there
My actions and loyalties for you are true
By this you must know I do care..."

And as I close my eyes, on this ship of all ships, safe from harm
I hear you murmur as you hold me gently, tenderly in your arms
Mari, I love you...
And still tonight
The stars and the moon sets in his hands…

The Gift

You were offered a gift:
But you refused the gift; did you think it had a cost?
The gift was free; the beautiful gift is now but a sad loss
The gift was unconditional, straight from my heart
I wanted to share memories with you and for your part

You had just to receive no strings, no burdens to your soul
Dreams, hopes, past and future, tied together as we got old
I knew your past, your thoughts, but life has changed your view
At one time I was your hope, now I can't even reach you

I feel the concern for others you know
The time, the effort to solve, the love you show
I listen about the children for whom you care
I smile at the fishing stories, wishing I could be there

You are an honorable man, so precious, so kind
I wish that you would share with me what is on your mind
In my life I have once loved deep
One so much but Him I couldn't keep

But now I know deep down in my heart
I long to be with you, to be a part
Of the man you are and the life you lead
To be a part of your hurdles, meet your needs

But you refuse to let me over the wall
You keep me at a distance, not giving me your all
A person can only hold on so long
One day you turn around and they are gone

All I wanted was:

To be a comfort in time of need
Be a help to you in time of heed
Be there to love you through thick and thin
When you are sad, for you to let me begin

Lifting your spirits and make you smile
Holding your next to my soul all the while
You're a man of character; your strength is your word
Stubborn, but never a bad comment about you is heard

You have a choice of the gifts in life you receive
You have the choice on how just to perceive
Your life was presented with a gift, but were you to blind to see
That the gift was within your reach was freely given...
The gift was love.... The gift was me....

Yellow Brick Road

I hopped along a yellow brick road
In oversized ruby clogs
The Bunk & Belly Inn I was told
Is a place that welcomes frogs

Storms snatched me from paradise
My stagnant lily pond
I am told that good Queen Cape
Lives in a pond beyond

She will return me to home I am told
To the place where I come from
For she is a piper wise and fair
Who shades beneath a leafy palm

Though I have never seen her
Fabulous tales of her perfume the air
She is a legend in her own time
And those honest fall into her care

I hopped along this golden road
Exhausted from my quest
But my home strained until my return
Until returned I could not rest

On the first part of my trip
I met a lively ape
He was vaulting all about
Searching for good Queen Cape

"Will you go with me," I asked
When he finally settled still
"No you silly frog," he said
You shall become road kill."

I will swing my way through trees
To the Bunk & Belly Inn

You hop along your road
I doubt our paths will cross again

I watched him swing quickly through trees
How I envied this monkey's grin
If I could scale the highest tree
Perhaps I could glimpse home again

Hop along I did awhile
I was not to be undone
Tedious was my grounded route
But I would finish the task begun

My polliwogs relied on me
They must miss me by now
Ruby clogs are my one hope
They were blessed by a sacred cow

Soon I crossed a raven
With glasses on his eyes
He made a feast of carrion
While I feasted on flies

Do you know the way?
To the Bunk &Belly Inn
I have lost my way back
To my charming pungent fen

What you need my web footed friend
Are glasses so you can see
Give me your ruby clogs
And I will give you these

Toto… Where are you?

Choose Life

Woefully strained and vivacity drained
I arranged to shed despair and bide
Through each sight viewed had perdition imbued
Into sleep's care I must direct my stride
      Shutter sheer windows and lock away light
      Enter fear's bog of fog-darkened fright

Retreat from live heat that scorched this day's meat
I notice road dust soil my worthless shoes
Quake when I see footprints following me
Worn sole's errors no breast would excuse
      Lo! Blistering snaps my old ears have known
      Thus through sad nights with dull woe do I groan

I bend my raw back and let fall my pack
Crack my sore spine to allay worldly woes
Pray the addle yoke is with dream keys broke
And dream fiends trudge past in peaceable rows
      Huddled alone I recall what I've feared
      My bulk, faculties, and spirit cashiered

Air knives start in twos butchering my blues
Current woes and bygone troubles combined
Soon I am entombed as more monsters wound
Damning screams broil my flash flooded mind
      Around and around like bees they swarm
      Stoking my brain to keep their outrage warm

A screeching sprite trills in callow delight
He often wiles this shadowy moor I rove
And all these long whiles ruthlessly beguiles
Mocks as he bodes forth my ignoble trove
      It is through deep sleep that he ambles most
      Hounds me often to forfeit my vexed ghost

Lo, woeful strains freeze like ice in my veins
Sweet sleep lounges on the lakeshore of doom
Sleep sheep slaughtered, their woolen robes watered
Laments I raise foul air like filthy fume
      Oh that they had grazed in a pensive dell
      These lambs might have eschewed death's lurid knell

Thor's swift hammer raised a pounding clamor
Bloody bastards found humor and laughed
Doomed archers roar, then let their arrows sore
Piercing my muse with each murderous shaft
      Lo! Another night these demons choke rest
      Heavy in my soul, heavier in my breast

While lying back, fleet falls their attack
Comes they to shine fool's fire upon what's past
And my thin shield, how quickly it does yield
As though my scant mirth were beggar's repast
      Why does what I hold in a wee amount
      Bring them to feast as though fed on the mount?

Blunt club of Thor, pray calm your thunderous roar!
Pass me over this night and stand at bay
And you cruel sprites how find you such delights?
Damn! Find another yard where you could play!
      Fouler than foul why came you unto me
      I'd tie you not to my worst enemy!

But it soon rang clear that they'd not quit here
Until their course was most completely run
I try to pray. For what I cannot say
As it was something I had never done
      Tortured, tormented, surrounded by dread
      Harsh murderous noise pounds my leaden head

'Cross inky ash tore a bright lightning slash
By which saw I knelt in a roiling fen
As if spell-bound, time silenced bestial sound
Which retreated into a horrid den
      Dire and ill-omened rolled a fiery wheel
      That breath from my lungs did violently steal

Then in a rush dismal clamor did hush
Quickly threshing the wispy grain of life
Slashing through gloom came suffocating doom
That pared life's thread with a death-sharpened knife
      Not a stir, nor sound, nor whispering breeze
      No scent nor sight nor lung-laboring wheeze

Tried I to shout; beg Christ pray let me out!
Derision froze the breath inside my throat
Else my deafened ear could no longer hear
In my life's song this seemed a fade out note
      Darkness, darkness; stinking pitch robbing 'round
      Quiet, Quiet, Christ I am hell-ward bound!

Though barred from defense, felt I had all sense
Which heaped torment onto dreadful dismay
Groped I in pitch dark, probing for a spark
That might cast light on my dreary pathway
      Shortly I fathomed cold horror most sure
      My mind could never have conceived before

Like day's first show I glimpsed a distant glow
Toward will o' the wisp my daunted soul drew
Doom I deny and cruel conduct defy
But as if me to gall, onward I flew
      I bellow and bark but fell ears don't hear
      Arise mortal mate; perdition looms near!

Prodding headlong toward punishment for wrong
Concede I have no choice but to amend
For when I could choose my life I would loose
Before I would onto pensive knees bend
        Lived life as I would rather rule in hell
        Than serve heaven when for me tolled the bell

As I drew nearer sorrows grew clearer
My wrongs before dead eyes were brought to bear
From my first breath till my moment of death
Each scorn I'd born was weighed against all care
        While being judged saw how I had wasted days
        Mild morns in slumber, dismal days in haze

Through dull eyes of mine God's light could not shine
Now my soul shall tinder a lava flow
Why? Why did I fright, when given pure light?
Now I am thrown where only fear can grow
        Lo! Sorrow grows as misery speeds my flight
        Wake, mortal partner, from this fatal night!

Miasmatic smoke makes my soul's lungs choke
I have sight and smell and vision it seemed
But I had not heard a whispering word
But something touched me; or had I but dreamed?
        Horror! I feel heat from the burning lake
        Why am I here? This is all a mistake!

Twas never a time I committed a crime
Nor did I in pride or vanity gloat
Ne'er was jolly; thence what was my folly?
I only left my home to launch my boat
        Because I fished the wide ocean at noon
        Am I now condemned to the lake of doom?

Woeful, tragic day! God! Now I could pray
But why seemed virtue slippery in my grasp?
Doesn't evil fly when you evil deny?
I'm forced yet closer toward eternal clasp
        Savage pain awaits just beyond Styx' brim
        I pall as Phlegyas oars toward the rim

"Welcome dull swain," he whispered to my brain
 "We have a place reserved here just for you
Your wage for nights you reveled in delights
Feel free to revel in our deathless stew"
        Then he laughed loudly a hideous howl
        Then offered his hand and flaunted his scowl

Mystical Pens

My mind distressed over this harrowed rest
I am marked with the self same brand as Cain
I grasp what I've won for vile deeds I've done
Shake my head while recalling those I've slain
      My eyes at last opened while in death shut
      Quaking and shaking rolls my wretched gut

By my lying tongue were pious persons stung
A serpent's tooth could not have poisoned worse
Oh foul fiend look morose on what you've gleaned
Your derision has brought you to this curse
      The wise warned of these wages many times
      But I harkened not and wrought impious crimes

Lo! Torture waits inside those fettered gates
I hang my head and reach for Phlegyas' hand
Abjuring chance I might wake from this trance
I look once more back on cooling land
      My eyes take one last glance about for hope
      Always in agony; how do I cope?

As faith I forsook the hellish ground shook
His hand was not able to grapple mine
Turning I flew back through vacuous stew
Returning on that same despondent line
      I gave God thanks for this instant relief
      My horror great but my damnation brief

Then, unawares, I wakened on my stairs
Sweat pouring forth from every inch of skin
Sundry wiles seen through this pedantic dream
From base jokes to the most ignoble sin
      Many things in life to be ashamed of
      Why did I not in God's bosom find love?

I let my mind float as a sullen boat
Is it not true that decency can save?
Many I have chased while life waned in waste
Is this what I shall take into my grave?
      No. There must be a solution to this
      But where does one turn for moral guidance?

I largely chose wrong as life waxed along
Mine was the only counsel I would trust
Ethics would not hold while hell ward I rolled
I pined for pride and nefarious lust
      Oh, what a waste of notorious shame
      This world should be loath to recall my name

Was it not said in a book I once read?
That we are made in the image of God
Though life is brief his oath transcends belief
In his eyes unstained though our lives are flawed
      Would one who is divine master of all
      Actually hear my words if call?

Was it not his design that we should each shine?
Should we aim to find splendor during life?
The dull way is to hang our heads and pray
But this was what has caused my worldly strife
      Lo! How I trembled while hunched near the brink
      Those sights and smells would make Goliath shrink

In chills I rack recalling that attack
Something has to amend and that is sure
The bright light inside I shall no more hide
This night I strike out to hunt down my cure
      On pensive knees I down: hanging my head
      Is the dear lord merciful, as they've said?

Thence I called his name, in my heart he came
And told me he'd waited long on me
He said I'd been tried with those tears I've cried
That they had worked to make my mind ready
      He spoke as a kind father to his son
      And my first step toward heaven was done

Each day on the road I lighten my load
Though sometimes my decisions lead me wrong
I shall nevermore cower upon the floor
God's hand will write the notes in every song
      Satan's kingdom is upon hatred built
      But I tremble not, shrouded with God's quilt

It's taken some time to sort in my mind
But my father tells me I have earned his love
All I had to do was to tell my father true
That all things I must lift my lord above
      Life is much smoother with God standing guard
      Why did I think this sure deed was so hard?

Now I grace away each test sent my way
Evil tries to tempt me from my lord's side
But I am not fooled and am by God ruled
For once in life I have nothing to hide
      Though this world is with ungodly sin rife
      In all turns I take this son shall choose life

Saint Peter Heard the Bell

Silent now the rocker that creaked as she sat and sewed
Meditation smoothed her brow relaxing her daily load
Praises raised to heaven she often sang to ease despair
Silenced when god gave this lady golden wings to wear

A brand new star is shining in the southern sky tonight
Ignited by a spirit that heaven bathed in golden light
Wilted hands that once tucked her children into bed
Are holding hands with seraphim, just as Jesus said

Her feet walk on golden streets with saints and with our lord
Resplendent smiles abound while she enjoys heaven's reward
Her mansion is the spacious one on Lovely Lady Lane
She's now enjoys eternity to find greatness in love again

On her head God placed a jeweled crown of spotless gold
In her arms a lamb she has an eternity to hold
She walks beneath the splendor of God's guiding light
His glory she enjoys while we lock our doors at night

Devotion to God has taken her into his arms of love
Her voice is now as soothing as the cooing of a dove
She has won a victory while we pray at heaven's door
Praying for the time when we have cause to fear no more

Then let mortality take us for in death we eternity win
When we breathe for God on earth, in heaven we breathe again
The promise of God's grace smoothes our wrinkled shell
When dear Helen got her wings, Saint Peter answered the bell...

Your Solution

When your world becomes too complex to bear
And stars in your sky fall faster each hour
Siren's shrill scream fills every inch of air
Each face you look at turns your stomach sour
Take a few moments; examine your soul
Breathe a bit slower and think of a tree
For every hardship you attempt to control
Was struggled ten fold upon Calvary
Evil grasped firm to mute the son of man
To keep him from teaching God's children right
To keep him from spreading truth of God's plan
To imbue despair through winds of delight
      For though your life may be horribly flawed
      Your solution begins and ends with God

Selah

About Our Writers

Joel Morgan: Born May 26th, 1960 to a sailor, Theron Morgan and his wife Faye, at a time when America was in deep dismay over the actions of Fidel Castro and communist insurgents who seized control of the Cuban governmental machine. Thus his place of birth, although it happened on American soil, was recorded to be Cuba.

Joel is the 4th of 8 children and spent his youth in and around Charleston South Carolina. During his high school days he met is wife to be and the marriage that came of that meeting led Joel to Atlanta where he studied architecture and construction at Southern Technical Institute.

Joel later fathered two children with his wife who are his most influential stimulus. They are two of the most wonderful human beings you could ever hope to meet.

In the early 90s, Joel and his wife became foster parents and for three years helped to raise other children who were placed in risky environments by circumstances beyond their control. During their tenure as foster parents, Joel and Regina were awarded the honor of being named 'Foster Parents of the Year' in their home county of Douglas Georgia and were then awarded with the same honor for the state of Georgia as well. Raising children were something that Joel and his wife did well.

Separation and divorce led Joel back to South Carolina where he now lives and writes and worships his savior. Joel attends Summerbrook Community Church and is a member of The Poetry Society of South Carolina, and of the Summerville Writer's Guild.

Mari Scott: Born January 21 and raised southern, always dabbling around with a combination of words, mostly a journal that turned into a small novel. A creative imagination from a very early age, she was the one to always write the short skits, direct plays at school or make new lyrics for familiar songs.

The love of writing grew as she volunteered her time at camps and 43 local churches with children's mission programs. Writing poems as gifts to cherish love ones, teaching creative writing on the college level, using her love of poetry in Children's Church activities.

A published songwriter and poet, with three poetry books and a fiction book (Me, Brother-in-law and Uncle Pete) in progress about the joys of her beloved late brother.

Co-Chairman of Ninian's Poetry Cafe and Dallas Slam 2000-2001 and a Poetry Host for 2 years. Mari is the founder and owner of Poetry World in Spiral Matrix, and "The Poetry Café" in VooDoo Chat.

Mari lives near Chicago in a small suburban town that rest on Lake Michigan. She is the mother of one daughter, and will be a grandmother in May of this year.

Mystical Pens

www.ingramcontent.com/pod-product-compliance
Lightning Source LLC
Chambersburg PA
CBHW051707040426
42446CB00008B/754